Mastering Fi

for Video Editing

The Structured Approach to Editing Videos Professionally

Friedrich Marvin

ISBN: 9798282013740
Imprint: Independently published

TABLE OF CONTENTS

Filmora 14 is a video editing tool made for both beginners and professionals. It helps you work faster with a simple and easy-to-use interface, so you can focus more on being creative instead of worrying about complicated steps. With many tools like cool effects, smooth transitions, and sound editing, Filmora 14 makes it easy to create great-looking videos.

One of the best things about Filmora 14 is how user-friendly it is. You can just drag and drop your videos, pictures, and music into the timeline, which saves a lot of time. It also has a big collection of ready-made templates and effects that help make your videos look even better.

Filmora 14 supports many different file types and works well on different devices and platforms. Whether you're making videos for fun, social media, or YouTube, it gives you the right tools to bring your ideas to life. You can also use features like motion tracking, green screen, and editing from multiple cameras at once.

In short, Filmora 14 is more than just a video editing app — it's a creative tool that helps you make amazing videos with ease. Its powerful features and simple design make it perfect for anyone who wants to create something special.

Why Filmora Video Editor?

- It's very easy to use, making it great for both beginners and professionals.

- It includes powerful features like split-screen, speed control, and keyframe animation.
- Comes with lots of effects, transitions, and music to boost your creativity.
- Works with many file types and runs smoothly on different devices.
- Gives you professional tools at an affordable price.
- Perfect for all kinds of projects—events, marketing, education, and YouTube.
- Regular updates help your videos stay fresh and trendy.

This book is for

- **Content Creators:** Learn how to use Filmora to make amazing vlogs and tutorials.

- **Corporate Professionals:** Create clean, professional videos and presentations.

- **Digital Marketers:** Design attention-grabbing ads for social media.

- **Educators:** Make your lessons more fun and engaging with visual content.

- **Event Creators:** Put together beautiful highlight videos for special events.

- **Storytellers:** Make impressive short films without spending too much.

Where Should I Start?

Getting started with Filmora is simple, even if you're brand new to video editing. Just follow these easy steps:

Download and Install Filmora:

Go to the official Filmora website, download the latest version for your device, install it, and you're ready to begin.

Get to Know the Interface:

Open Filmora and look around. Learn where the timeline, preview window, and tools like transitions, effects, and audio controls are.

Try a Simple Project:

Import a video, photo, or audio file. Practice basic edits like trimming, cutting, and arranging clips on the timeline.

Use Tutorials and Guides:

Check out Filmora's built-in tips, YouTube tutorials, or user guides to learn how to use different features.

Play with Effects:

Add transitions, text, and filters. You can also adjust colors or try out fun tools like green screen or keyframing.

Save and Export Your Work:

When your video is ready, save your project and export it in the format you want. This helps you understand how to share your video.

Keep Practicing:

The more you use Filmora, the better you'll get. Start with small projects and build your skills as you go.

Start small, have fun exploring, and before long, you'll be creating videos that look polished and professional.

CHAPTER 1

A QUICK LOOK AT FILMORA VIDEO EDITING

It's amazing how far video editing has come. Today, you can easily edit and rearrange videos right on your computer or smartphone. But it wasn't always this simple. In the past, video editing was much harder—especially before non-linear editing (NLE) software came along. Back then, editing often meant just keeping the camera rolling until the right moment. That was it. Even basic cuts weren't understood or used widely.

Now, many boring and time-consuming editing tasks, like masking and adding captions, are being replaced by smart tools and automation. It's been a long journey for video editing, and over time, there have been many important improvements and milestones.

What makes editing software truly useful is both what it can do and how easy it is to use. The design of the user interface is a big deal. A well-designed interface makes editing smoother and more enjoyable. Some editing tools aren't very popular simply because their interface is hard to use.

Learning how to use the interface is just as important as learning how to use the features. When you understand how the interface works, everything else becomes easier. You can think of the interface like a map—if you can read the map, you can find your way around and edit your videos with confidence.

How Has Video Editing Evolved?

Video editing has come a long way thanks to technology. New tools, both hardware and software, have made editing much easier and more powerful. Here are some of the biggest changes in video editing over time:

11

1. Digital Editing:

Switching from analog to digital changed everything. Editors no longer needed physical film. They could now cut, move, and change clips right on a computer. This made editing faster, more flexible, and more creative.

2. Better Software Features:

Today's editing programs have many advanced tools. You can now add visual effects, adjust colors, and mix sound. Interfaces are also easier to use, so even beginners can learn to edit.

3. Real-Time Playback:

Thanks to better hardware and software, editors can now watch changes instantly—no need to wait for rendering. This makes editing quicker and helps you see your work as you go.

4. High-Resolution Videos:

With the rise of 4K and even 8K cameras and screens, editors can now work with super clear, high-quality videos. Editing software has been adapted to handle these large, detailed files.

5. Special Effects and Visual Enhancements:

Tools like motion tracking, green screen, and 3D effects are now easier to use. These features help editors create professional-looking videos with eye-catching results.

6. Cloud-Based Editing and Teamwork:

The cloud has made it possible for people to edit the same project from different places. Teams can share files, ideas, and feedback online. This makes working together easier and faster.

7. Faster Exporting and Rendering:

Modern editing software uses powerful tech to speed things up. Multi-threading and GPU acceleration help editors render and export videos more quickly, saving valuable time.

8. Support for More Formats and Tools:

Editing programs now work well with many file types and other software. You can use them with audio editors, effects tools, and more. This makes it easier to bring everything together in one project.

9. Mobile Editing:

Smartphones and tablets now have apps that let users edit on the go. This makes video editing easier and more convenient—perfect for people who need to create content anytime, anywhere.

10. AI-Powered Editing:

Artificial intelligence helps speed things up by automating boring tasks and giving smart suggestions. AI can learn your style and recommend changes, saving time and helping you stay creative.

Video editing today is more powerful, accessible, and exciting than ever before!

The Secret Ingredients of Top Video Editing Tools

1. **Easy to Use**
   A good editor should be simple to understand, with clear menus and buttons. This helps beginners and pros work faster without getting confused.
2. **Works with Many File Types**
   The software should open and save different kinds of video, audio, and image files, so you don't need to waste time converting formats.
3. **Great Video Tools**

It should let you cut, trim, join clips, and make all kinds of edits easily—whether you're doing something basic or more advanced.

4. **Strong Audio Controls**

   Good editing includes great sound. You should be able to fix the volume, sync audio with video, and add cool sound effects or music.

5. **Cool Effects and Filters**

   Adding filters, motion effects, text, and animations helps your video stand out and feel more creative and fun.

6. **Saves in High Quality**

   The software should let you save videos in HD, 4K, or even higher. You should also be able to choose the file size and format you want.

7. **Runs Smooth and Fast**

   It should play your edits smoothly and save your videos quickly, without freezing or slowing down your computer.

8. **Share and Work with Others**

   If you're working with a team or sharing videos online, the software should make that easy. Cloud features and teamwork tools help a lot.

9. **Fair Prices**

   The software should give you different ways to pay—like one-time purchases or monthly plans—so you can choose what works for your budget.

10. **Keeps Getting Better**

    A great tool updates often with new features and fixes. It should also have customer support when you need help.

What Makes Filmora a Great Video Editing Tool?

1. **All-in-One Editing Tools**

Filmora lets you do both simple and advanced video editing. Whether you're just starting or already creating YouTube content, it's got what you need.

2. **Easy to Use**

Its clean and simple design makes it easy for anyone to learn and use—no stress, even if you're new to editing.

3. **Works with Many File Types**

You can import and export all kinds of videos, sounds, and images like MP4, PAL, and JPEG. That means no worries about file compatibility.

4. **Edit in 4K**

Want super clear, high-quality videos? Filmora supports 4K resolution, so your videos can look amazing on any screen.

5. **Great Audio Tools**

You can add music or voiceovers from Filmora's built-in sound library or use your files. It's flexible and simple to control your audio.

6. **Faster Exports**

Updates have made Filmora quicker when it comes to saving your work. You won't have to wait long to finish and share your videos.

7. **Lots of Cool Effects**

Filmora comes packed with effects, transitions, and filters you can use to make your videos more fun, creative, or professional-looking.

8. **Custom Video Sizes**

You can easily change your video's shape or size to fit YouTube, Instagram, TikTok, or whatever platform you're using.

9. **Smart AI Tools**

Filmora keeps getting smarter! With built-in AI tools, you can let the software help with edits like removing backgrounds or syncing music.

10. Free and Paid Versions

You can start editing for free, or choose a paid plan for more features. It's flexible, so you only pay for what you need.

New Features in Filmora 14

1. Smart BGM Production:

Filmora's AI picks the best background music for your video based on its mood and content, saving you time picking music manually.

2. Filmora Copilot 2.0:

A smart assistant that helps you find resources, apply effects, and process things in batches while you edit.

3. Planar Monitoring:

This feature uses advanced 3D tracking to attach text, images, or videos to flat surfaces in your video, making everything look natural as the camera moves.

4. Multi-Camera Editing

Edit videos from different camera angles all in one timeline. It's easy to switch between views for smoother transitions and dynamic sequences.

5. Path Curve for Keyframes

Make your animations flow smoothly with better keyframe controls. You can now create more fluid motion paths for video elements.

6. AI Face Mosaic

Automatically blur faces for privacy or stylistic purposes by tracking facial movements in your videos.

7. AI-Powered Video Enhancer

Boost the quality of blurry or low-resolution videos using cloud-based AI. It improves clarity and restores lost details.

8. Video Noise Reduction

Reduce grain and noise in videos taken in low light or with high ISO, making them sharper and clearer.

9. **AI Color Palette**

   Match your video's color scheme to a reference image or video for a professional, cinematic look while keeping natural skin tones.

10. **AI Voice Enhancer**

    Clear up voice recordings by removing background noise, making voices sound cleaner and more professional.

11. **AI Lip Sync**

    Automatically sync lip movements to speech, making translations look more natural and realistic.

12. **AI Portrait Cutout**

    Remove backgrounds more accurately, including tricky details like hair, for a cleaner, sharper result.

13. **AI Sound Effects Generator**

    Create custom sound effects by simply describing them in text. The AI will generate the sound for you.

14. **Magnetic Timeline**

    Organize clips easily with an automatic snapping feature that makes aligning and editing tracks faster.

15. **Advanced Compression**

    Reduce video file sizes without losing quality, making it easier to share and store your videos.

16. **Smart Scene Cut**

    Let the AI detect the best moments in your footage and automatically cut out unnecessary parts, focusing on faces and key objects.

17. **Smart Short Videos**

    Automatically divide longer videos into short clips perfect for social media. The AI picks out highlights and turns them into vertical videos with music and subtitles.

Filmora 14 System Requirements

Filmora 14 is a powerful video editing software, but to make sure it runs smoothly on your computer, you'll need to meet certain system requirements. These are the minimum specs your computer should have to use Filmora 14 without any issues. Let's take a look at what you need to get started!

For Windows:

1. **Operating System**: Windows 7, 8.1, 10, or 11 (64-bit only)
2. **Processor**: Intel i3 or better, 2GHz or faster (Intel 6th Gen or newer is best for HD/4K editing)
3. **RAM**: 8 GB (16 GB is better for HD/4K videos)
4. **Graphics**:
   - Intel HD 5000 or newer
   - NVIDIA GeForce GTX 700 or newer
   - AMD Radeon R5 or newer
   - (2 GB VRAM, 4 GB is better for HD/4K)
5. **Storage**: 10 GB of free space (SSD is recommended for HD/4K content)
6. **Internet**: Needed to activate and use online services

For macOS:

1. **Operating System**: macOS 10.15 (Catalina) to macOS 15 (Sequoia)
2. **Processor**: Intel i5 or better, 2GHz or faster (Intel 6th Gen or newer is best for HD/4K, Apple M3 chip works too)
3. **RAM**: 8 GB (16 GB is better for HD/4K videos)
4. **Graphics**:
   - Intel HD 5000 or newer
   - NVIDIA GeForce GTX 700 or newer
   - AMD Radeon R5 or newer

- (2 GB VRAM, 4 GB is better for HD/4K)

5. **Storage**: 10 GB of free space (SSD is recommended for smoother HD/4K editing)

6. **Internet**: Needed for registration and online services

GPU and Driver Requirements for Filmora (Windows)

To get the best performance with Filmora, here's what your system should have:

1. **Processor**: Intel i3 or higher, 2GHz or faster (For HD/4K videos, it's best to have Intel 6th Gen or newer)
2. **Operating System**: A 64-bit version of Windows 7, 8.1, 10, or 11
3. **RAM**: At least 8 GB (For HD/4K videos, 16 GB is recommended)
4. **Graphics Card (GPU)**: At least 2 GB of GPU memory

GPU Accelerated Rendering

GPU acceleration helps speed up the editing process by letting your GPU handle some of the workload. This makes video playback smoother and reduces lag, so your editing experience is quicker and more efficient.

How to Turn on GPU Acceleration

1. Open **File** and go to **Preferences**.

2. Click on the **Performance** tab.

3. Tick the box that says **Enable Hardware Acceleration for video rendering and playback**.

4. If you'd like to speed up video decoding, tick the box below it too.

Tech Specifications

Supported Input Formats in Filmora

Filmora supports a wide variety of formats, making it easy to import and edit videos from different sources. Here are some of the main formats it can handle:

Video Formats:

1. AV1 (.av1): A modern format known for its high-quality compression.
2. AVI (.avi): A popular video format developed by Microsoft.
3. Camcorder Files (.dv, .tod, .mod, .mts, .m2ts, .m2t): Common formats used by digital camcorders.
4. FLV/F4V (.flv, .f4v): Older formats once used for online videos, especially on older websites.
5. HTML5 Video (.webm, .mp4, .ogv): Formats used for web-based video playback.
6. MKV (.mkv): A flexible format that supports multiple video and audio tracks.
7. MPEG-1/2 (.mpeg, .mpg, .m1v, .m2v): Older formats used for DVDs and digital broadcasting.

8. MPEG-4 (.m4v, .mp4, .3g2, .3gp, .3gp2): A widely supported format for mobile devices, streaming, and high-quality videos.
9. Non-Encrypted DVD Files (.vob, .vro): Used for DVD video content without encryption.
10. QuickTime (.mov): A format common on Apple devices that supports MPEG-4 or MJPEG encoding.
11. WMV/ASF (.wmv, .asf): A format developed by Microsoft, often used for Windows-based media playback.

These formats allow Filmora to work with a broad range of video and audio sources.

Audio Formats:

- Filmora supports a wide range of audio file formats including .mp3, .m4a, .wav, .wma, .oga, .ogg, .flac, .aif, and .aiff.

Image Formats:

- You can import and work with various image file types such as .svg, .jpg, .png, .bmp, .gif, .tif, and .tiff.

Output Formats:

Video/Audio Formats:

- Filmora offers flexibility with its output options, supporting popular formats like .mp4, .wmv, .avl, .hevc, .avi, .mov, GoPro Cineform, .f4v, .mkv, .ts, .3gp, .mpeg-2, .webm, as well as image sequences (.png, .jpg), and audio files (.mp3, .wav).

4K Video Output:

- For 4K video editing, Filmora supports the following formats: .mp4, .mov, and .mkv.

Device and Social Network Profiles:

- **Devices:** Filmora is compatible with various devices, including iPhone, iPad, Apple TV, Apple TV 4K, iPod, Samsung Galaxy, Google Pixel, Android devices, Xbox One, PlayStation 4, PSP, and Smart TVs.

- **Social Networks:** Directly share to platforms like YouTube, Vimeo, and TikTok with Filmora's optimized settings.

DVD Formats:

- You can also export to DVD formats, including DVD, DVD folder, and ISO disc image files.

These format options provide great flexibility for both editing and exporting videos across a range of devices and platforms.

What You'll Discover from This Book

Let's be honest—video editing can feel overwhelming when you're just starting. So many tools, timelines, and buttons... where do you even begin?

That's exactly why this book exists.

Whether you've never opened a video editor before or you've played around with a few clips and now want to step up your game, this guide is for *you*. It's not packed with jargon or complex theories—just real, easy-to-follow tips that help you turn your creative ideas into polished videos using **Wondershare Filmora 14**.

Here's a sneak peek of what's waiting for you inside:

- **A simple breakdown of how video editing has changed— and why Filmora stands out.** You'll learn what makes it such a go-to tool for beginners and pros alike.

- **A friendly tour of Filmora's workspace.** No more clicking around randomly—get to know the layout, tools, and features that matter for your projects.

- **Tips for making Filmora feel like your own.** Customize the layout, improve playback, organize your clips—whatever helps your editing flow better.

- **Step-by-step editing techniques.** You'll learn how to cut, trim, zoom, split, and layer like a pro—even if you've never edited a video before.

- **Creative shortcuts and time-saving hacks.** Want to use cool effects, speed up or slow down clips, or throw in fun stickers and text? We'll show you how (and make it fun!).

- **All things audio.** Good sound makes a huge difference. We'll help you add music, adjust volume, sync audio with your video, and even convert voice to text.

- **A taste of Filmora's smart AI tools.** Let the software help you with scene cuts, highlight reels, and turning photos into slick videos—so you can focus on creativity.

Think of this book as your editing buddy—someone sitting next to you, showing you what to click, when to do it, and why it matters. No pressure, no stress—just real guidance to help you create videos you're proud of.

By the end, you won't just *know* how to use Filmora. You'll feel *confident* using it to tell your story, promote your brand, or just have fun being creative.

Understanding How to Use This Book

This book is your complete guide to learning Wondershare Filmora. To get the best experience, here's how to use it effectively:

1. **Start Where You Feel Comfortable:** If you're new to video editing or Filmora, begin with the first chapters to learn the basics. If you already know a bit about editing, feel free to jump to the more advanced chapters.

2. **Practice Along the Way:** Each chapter has exercises for you to try. Don't just read—take the time to practice the tips and tricks. Learning by doing is the best way to improve.

3. **Use the Table of Contents:** The Table of Contents is like a map. If you need a quick reminder on a certain topic, you can easily find it. It's perfect for when you need specific information fast.

4. **Play Around with the Software:** Filmora has a lot of cool features. While you read, take the time to explore them yourself. The more you experiment, the more comfortable you'll get with the software.

5. **Don't Rush:** Video editing takes time to learn. Don't hurry through the chapters. Make sure you understand each step before moving on. You can always go back to earlier sections if you need a refresher.

6. **Check the Glossary and Index:** If you come across any confusing terms, look them up in the Glossary at the end of the book. The Index is also helpful for finding specific topics quickly.

7. **Bookmark Important Chapters:** Some chapters, like those on advanced features and audio editing, will be useful for you to revisit often. You can mark them so you can easily find them when working on your projects.

8. **Use Bonus Resources:** At the end of the book, you'll find extra tools like keyboard shortcuts and tips to help you get the most out of Filmora. These will make editing faster and easier.

CHAPTER 2

GETTING SET UP WITH FILMORA

Starting your video editing journey with Filmora is an exciting step! Whether you're a complete beginner or have some experience, Filmora is designed to make editing easy and fun. With a simple, intuitive interface, it's perfect for getting things done quickly while still offering powerful tools for more advanced projects. In this section, we'll walk you through downloading and installing Filmora, then take you on a tour of its user-friendly interface. By the end, you'll feel confident navigating the software and ready to dive into your first project. Let's get started!

Downloading the Software

1. Go to https://filmora.wondershare.com.
2. On the homepage, choose the download option that matches your operating system (Windows or macOS). The setup file will automatically start downloading to your computer.

Once the download is complete, you're ready to move on to the installation!

3. Find the setup file in your *Downloads* folder and double-click it to start the installation.
4. A pop-up window will appear. Click Install.

5. Choose the installation location (or leave it as the default) and wait for the installation to complete. It should take a few minutes.

6. Once the installation is finished, open Filmora by double-clicking the icon on your desktop or clicking Start Now.

7. If you have a license, click Register and enter your license key.

8. On the login screen, enter your Wondershare ID (the email you used to purchase the software) and password.

9. If you don't have an account, you can sign up using Facebook, Google+, or Twitter.

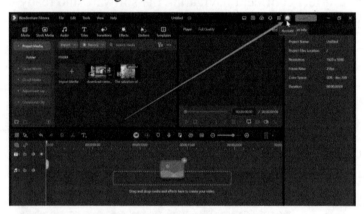

Note: If you don't have a Wondershare ID yet, you can easily create one on the official Filmora website:

- Go to https://filmora.wondershare.com
- Click the Sign In button at the top of the page to open the login panel
- From there, follow the steps to create a new account.

- You can try Filmora for free, but your videos will have a watermark unless you buy the full version.

- To make a new account, click *Create an Account* and fill out the form to sign up.

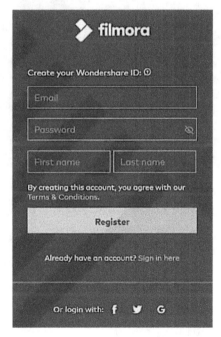

- Once Filmora is fully open, click the account icon in the top right corner to continue.

- After you log in, click the profile picture (avatar) to check if your account is activated.

- To keep Filmora up to date, you can check for updates manually or let the software do it for you.

To turn on automatic updates, just follow these steps:

1. Click on the File menu at the top of the screen and select Preferences.
2. In the preferences window, look for the Check for updates automatically option.
3. Choose how often you want Filmora to check for updates: Never, Daily, Weekly, or Monthly—whatever works best for you.

4. If a new update is available, a Live Update window will pop up when you open Filmora. Just click Update Now to start the update.

5. Once the update finishes downloading, click YES to close Filmora and install the latest version. Or, if you prefer to do it later, click Cancel and it will update the next time you open the program.

6. If you don't want to be asked about updates automatically, set Check for Updates to Never in the Preferences.

7. You can also manually check for updates anytime by going to the Help menu and clicking Check for Update.

To avoid losing your work, make sure to manually save your project before updating Filmora.

Getting to Know filmora's Workspace

Filmora is designed to make video editing easy and enjoyable, whether you're just getting started or already have some experience. Its clean layout and simple tools help you find everything you need without feeling overwhelmed.

Let's take a quick tour of the key parts of filmora's workspace:

- **Media Panel**: This is where all your photos, videos, and audio files are stored. You can organize your files here before adding them to your project.
- **Main Screen**: This is the central area where most of your editing happens.
- **Preview Window**: Want to see how your edits look? This window lets you watch your video as you work on it.
- **Timeline**: Here's where you arrange your clips in order—like putting puzzle pieces together to build your final video.
- **Effects & Transitions Panel**: Add cool effects, filters, and smooth transitions between clips to make your video more fun and professional.
- **Toolbar**: Gives you quick access to important tools like cutting, trimming, and more.
- **Export Panel**: When your video is ready, this is where you go to save and share it.
- **Audio Mixer**: Helps you adjust volume levels and sound quality to make your video sound great.
- **Project Details Pane**: Shows key info about your current project so you can stay organized.

Each of these parts works together to help you edit your videos easily and creatively. From the moment you import your files to the final step of exporting your video, Filmora gives you everything you need in one smooth, easy-to-use space.

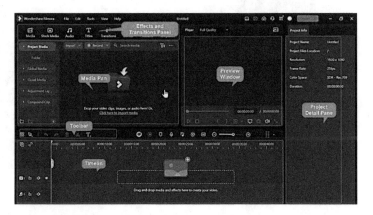

Filmora Main Screen

The main screen of Filmora is where you'll find everything you need to start and work on your video projects. It's designed to be simple and easy to navigate.

- **New Project Tab**: Located right on the main screen, this tab lets you start a new project with different editing options.

- **Aspect Ratio Selection**: Here, you can choose the right video dimensions for your project, making sure it fits your needs.

- **Creator Hub Tab**: Found in the left panel, this tab gives you more control over your workspace and project options.

- **Search Icon**: Need to find an old project? This icon helps you quickly search and open past projects.

- **Filmora Cloud**: This feature lets you store, sync, and access your projects across different devices, making it easier to collaborate and keep everything in one place.

Filmora Media Panel

The Media Panel in Filmora is where you manage and import all your media files—photos, videos, and audio clips. You can easily drag and drop files into the panel, organize them into folders, and preview them before adding them to your timeline. If you're using multiple devices, Filmora also lets you import media from cloud services.

Here's what you'll find in the Media Panel:

- **Import Button**: This allows you to bring in files from cloud storage, mobile devices, cameras, or your PC.
- **Folders**: Organize your media into folders for easy access while editing.
- **Media Preview Window**: Preview your media files before placing them in the timeline.
- **Audio, Video, and Image Tabs**: These tabs help you filter your imported media by type—audio, video, or images.

- **Search Bar**: Quickly find specific files in your media library.

This panel makes it easy to manage your media, keep things organized, and stay efficient while editing!

Your Editing Playground (The Timeline)

This is where the real magic happens! The timeline is the place where you arrange and edit your videos, photos, audio, and effects.

Here's why it's awesome:

- You can stack multiple layers of video, audio, and effects to create exactly what you want.
- It's super easy to move clips around, cut them, and add transitions right where you need them.
- You also have access to advanced tools like keyframes if you want to take your editing a step further.

Think of the timeline as your creative workspace—it's simple, flexible, and gives you full control over how your video comes together.

What You'll See on the Timeline

The timeline is where you do most of your editing, and here are the main things you'll find there:

- **Playhead**: This is the vertical line that shows where you are in your video. You can drag it to move around and see different parts.
- **Snapping**: Makes editing easier by helping clips snap into place when you drag them close together—great for smooth transitions.
- **Time Ruler**: This sits at the top of the timeline and shows the time to help you line up your clips accurately.
- **Track Lock/Mute**: You can lock a track to avoid accidental changes or mute it if you don't want to hear the audio while working.
- **Tracks**: These are your editing layers for videos, music, effects, and text. You can stack and mix them as needed.
- **Zoom In/Out**: This lets you zoom in to edit details or zoom out to see the full project layout.

Preview Window – See Your Edits in Action

The Preview Window is the little screen in the top right corner where you watch your video as you edit. Every change you make on the timeline shows up here, so you can instantly see how things are looking. You can even play it in full screen and adjust the quality if your computer slows down.

Here's what you'll find in the Preview Window:

- **Playback Controls**: Buttons to play, pause, rewind, or fast-forward your video.

- **Frame Stepper**: This lets you move forward or backward one frame at a time—perfect for making tiny, precise edits.

- **Full-Screen Button**: Click this to view your video in full screen for a better look.

- **Playback Quality**: Lower the video quality while editing to avoid lag, especially if your computer is running slow.

- **Snapshot Button**: Takes a screenshot of whatever is on the screen at that moment—handy for thumbnails or saving a still.

- **Time Indicator**: Shows the exact time of the video frame you're currently watching or editing.

Inside the Effects & Transitions Panel in Filmora

Filmora makes it super easy to add fun effects and smooth transitions to your video clips. Whether you want to add a cool filter, fix colors, or fade from one scene to the next, you can do it all with just a drag and drop. The Effects and Transitions panels are your creative playground!

Here's what you'll find:

- **Effects Tab**: This is where you'll find all the fun visual effects—like filters, overlays, and cool distortions—to spice up your video.
- **Transitions Tab**: This lets you add smooth moves between scenes like fades, wipes, and slides.
- **Categories**: Everything is grouped by style (like cinematic, retro, 3D), so it's easy to find the look you want.
- **Search Bar**: If you already know the name of a transition or effect, just type it in here to find it fast.
- **Favorites**: Save the effects and transitions you use often so you can grab them quickly next time.

Getting to Know the Filmora Toolbar

The Toolbar sits right above your timeline and gives you quick access to the most important editing tools. Instead of digging through menus, you can do things like cutting clips, changing speed, adjusting audio, and more—right from one place. It helps you work faster and makes editing easier.

Here are the main tools you'll find:

- **Cut/Split Tool**: Use this to slice your video or audio clips into smaller parts. Great for removing the bits you don't want.
- **Crop Tool**: Want to focus on a certain part of your video? This lets you trim away the edges and keep just what matters.
- **Speed Adjustment**: Make your video play slower or faster with this tool—perfect for slow-motion or time-lapse effects.
- **Undo/Redo Buttons**: Did you make a mistake or want to go back? Just click undo. Change your mind again? Hit redo.
- **Zoom Controls**: These let you zoom in or out on the timeline so you can see more details or get a bigger picture of your whole project.

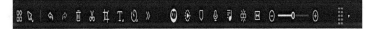

Filmora Project Info Panel:

The Project Detail Pane (or as we like to call it, the "Project Info Panel") shows you all the key details about your video project—like how long it is, the video quality, resolution, and more. It helps you stay organized and make changes easily, especially if you're editing for different platforms like YouTube, Instagram, or TikTok.

Here's what you'll find in this panel:

- **Project Name**: Want to stay organized? You can rename your project here so it's easy to find later.

- **Duration**: This tells you how long your entire video is—super helpful for timing things out just right.

- **Resolution & Frame Rate**: Check or change your video's quality and smoothness. Want it in 1080p at 30fps? You can set that here.

- **Aspect Ratio**: Shows your video's shape (like 16:9 for YouTube or 9:16 for TikTok). Helps make sure it fits perfectly on the platform.

- **Media Used**: See a list of all the photos, videos, and music you've added to your project so far.

- **File Path**: This shows where your project is saved on your computer—handy for keeping everything organized.

Export Panel: Share Your Video with the World

Once you've finished your project, the Export Panel is where you'll go to save and share your masterpiece. You can easily export your video in different file formats, share it directly to platforms like YouTube, Vimeo, and TikTok, or even burn it to a DVD. Filmora gives you the flexibility to choose the best settings for your project, whether it's for a social media upload or a personal device.

Here's what you'll find in the Export Panel:

- **Export Format Options**: Choose from different file formats (like MP4, MOV, AVI) and video resolutions to match your needs.
- **Device Presets**: Quick export settings for specific devices like smartphones, tablets, and game consoles—perfect for when you're sharing on different platforms.
- **Platform Export**: Directly upload to YouTube, Vimeo, TikTok, and other social sites, so your video can go live instantly.
- **Quality Settings**: Adjust the video quality for a balance between clear visuals and file size. If you're an advanced user, you can fine-tune bit rates, frame rates, and more with the Custom Export Settings.
- **Save Location**: See where your exported file will be saved on your device, making it easy to find.
- **Estimated File Size**: This shows an estimate of how big your video file will be based on your chosen settings.

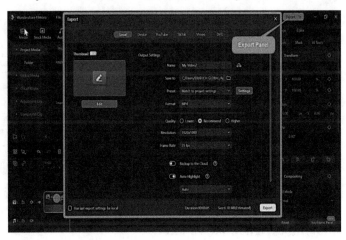

The Filmora Audio Mixer

The Audio Mixer helps you fine-tune all the sounds in your project, whether it's background music, voiceovers, or sound effects. You can adjust the balance, and volume, and even apply audio effects, giving you full control over how your project sounds. This ensures everything comes together with perfect audio quality.

Here's what you can do with the Audio Mixer:

- **Volume Controls**: Adjust the volume of each audio track with easy-to-use sliders.
- **Balance Control**: Change the balance between the left and right audio channels to get the right stereo feel.
- **Mute/Solo Buttons**: Mute or isolate a specific track while you're working, so you can focus on what matters most.
- **Audio Effects**: Add effects like reverb, noise reduction, and equalization to enhance your sound.
- **Master Track Volume**: Control the overall volume for your project with the master track slider.

This tool gives you the ability to perfect the sound of your video to match your vision!

Exploring the Elements Panel

The Elements Panel is like your creative toolbox. It holds different folders filled with content you've used or can use in your video. These include things like your own media, sample colors, green screen clips, shared assets, and even your photo library. Whether you're editing or starting fresh, this panel helps you quickly find and work with the visual elements that bring your video to life.

Media Section Made Simple

The Media section is where all your video ingredients live. It includes folders like Project Media, Shared Material, Sample Colors, Sample Videos, Green Screen clips, and your Photos Library. These folders store the content you've already used, are currently working with, or can use in your future projects. It's your go-to place for finding, organizing, and managing everything you need to build your video.

The Filmora Stock Media – Your Built-in Library of Visuals

The Stock Media tab gives you a bunch of ready-made images, videos, and effects you can use to level up your video. It's kind of like the My Media tab but filled with extra stuff from places like Pixabay, Unsplash, and Giphy. You'll also see folders like Favorites and Downloads to help you stay organized. Just drag and drop anything you like right into your project—no need to leave Filmora!

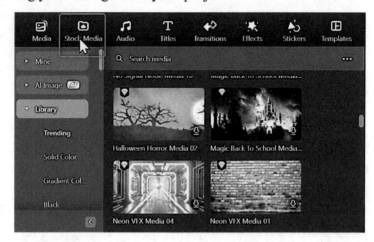

Filmora Audio Feature: Add Music and Sound to Your Video

The Audio tab lets you add background music and soundtracks to your video. It has a bunch of categories to choose from—like Beat Music, Travel, Vlogs, Electronic, Young & Bright, and more. If you find a track you like, you can save it to your Favorites for quick access later. Just drag the audio onto your timeline and you're good to go!

Using Titles in Filmora – Add Text Easily

The Titles feature in Filmora lets you add and customize different types of text, like titles, subtitles, headers, lower thirds, and end credits.

To get started, just pick the type of title you want. It'll show up in the Preview Window as a Title Box. Click inside that box to type your text. You can also choose a text style from the list on the left to change how it looks. It's that simple!

Using Transitions in Filmora – Smoothly Connect Your Clips

The Transitions feature in Filmora helps you connect two video clips with style. Inside the Transitions tab, you'll find a variety of animated effects that make the change from one clip to the next look smooth and visually appealing. Just drag and drop your favorite transition between clips to instantly enhance the flow of your video.

Using Filmora Effects – Add Style to Your Videos

The *Effects* panel in Filmora lets you easily add eye-catching visuals to your video clips. You can try out a variety of effects like overlays, fade-ins, flickers, AI stickers, portrait effects, scar lines, and more. These tools help you enhance your video's look and feel with just a few clicks—making your edits more fun, stylish, and professional.

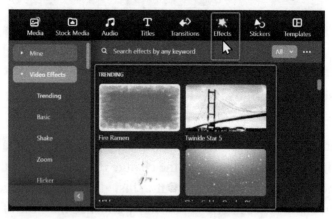

Using Filmora Stickers – Add Fun and Personality to Your Videos

The Stickers feature in Filmora lets you add both still and animated graphics to your videos. Whether you're trying to make your video more fun, highlight a specific moment, or just add some creative flair, Filmora has a big collection of customizable stickers to choose from. They're great for grabbing attention and giving your content a playful or expressive touch.

The Filmora Templates – Quick and Easy Video Creation

Filmora offers pre-made templates to help simplify the editing process. These templates come with ready-to-use layouts, effects, and transitions, allowing you to create professional-looking videos without starting from scratch. They're perfect for anyone looking for a fast, clean result with minimal effort.

CHAPTER 3

CUSTOMIZING THE FILMORA INTERFACE LAYOUT

This section covers the different layout options in Filmora, letting you adjust the workspace to suit your editing needs. Whether you want the default setup, more room for media, or a layout that works with two screens, these choices help you work more efficiently.

Layout Modes in Filmora

Filmora offers six different layout modes to suit your editing style. Here are the options:

1. **Default:** Restores the layout to its original panel setup.
2. **Organize:** Expands the media panel to the bottom of the screen.
3. **Edit:** Enlarges the property panel to the bottom of the screen.
4. **Short Video:** Perfect for creating vertical, short-form videos.
5. **Classic:** Offers the original look and feel of Filmora's first release.
6. **Dual:** Ideal for users with dual monitors for a more spacious workspace.

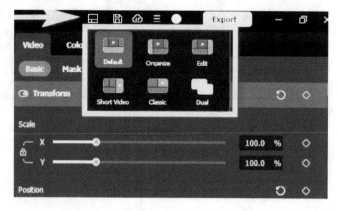

Resizing Panel Groups in Filmora

If you want to resize any of the panels to fit your needs, simply drag the resizing icon at the edges between panels. Here's how:

- Hover your pointer over the side of the panel until it turns into a left-and-right arrow. Then, drag it horizontally to resize.
- Hover your pointer below the panel until it turns into an up-and-down arrow. Then, drag it vertically to resize.

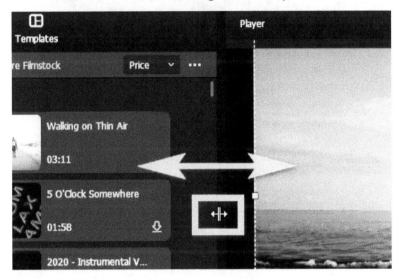

Witching Between Dark and Light Mode

To change between Dark and Light modes:

1. Go to File > Preferences > General.
2. Under Appearance, pick either Light Mode or Dark Mode.
3. Click OK to save your choice.

The Light Mode Should be exactly like this:

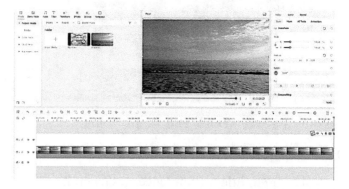

Note: If you choose *System Default,* the program's skin tone will match the color scheme of your operating system.

Filmora Project Settings

To change the basic settings for your project before you begin editing your video, go to File > Project Settings at the top of the screen.

Filmora offers intuitive controls that make trimming, splitting, and merging clips a breeze. You can easily enhance your videos with filters, transitions, and overlays to give them a clean, professional finish. The timeline view lets you manage multiple layers of audio and video with precision, making complex edits more manageable. When you're ready to share, you can upload directly to your favorite social media platforms with just a few clicks. Whether you're just getting started or already experienced, Filmora gives you the creative tools you need to bring your vision to life.

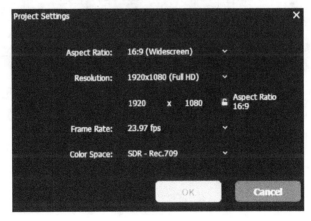

Setting Preferences

To make Filmora work best for you, you can adjust preferences related to appearance, folders, editing, and more. Here's what you can do:

- Change how Filmora looks, including adjusting the brightness of the interface and setting the default duration for transitions.
- Most preferences stay the same unless you decide to change them. However, the scratch disk settings you choose are saved with your project.
- When you open a project, the scratch disk settings you selected earlier will automatically be applied.

You can adjust settings for Folders, Editing, General, Save, and Performance. Once you're done customizing, click "OK" to apply the changes.

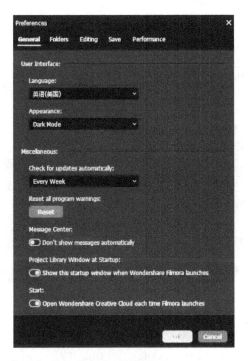

Adjusting Playback Quality in Filmora

To make editing smoother, you can change the playback quality in the Preview window. For better performance, you can use proxy media files, which are lower-resolution versions of your clips. This makes editing faster, and when you're done, you can export the full-size video.

Note: Proxy files are smaller and easier to work with because they have less data. With Filmora, you can edit using these proxy files and then export the high-quality video when you're finished.

Here's how it works:

- If Filmora notices any lag, it will suggest lowering the playback quality.
- Reducing the playback quality can help remove lag and save time while you edit.

To change the playback quality, just click the quality control menu and pick one of the options.

Here are the playback quality options you can choose from:

- **Finished**: View your video in preview mode without changing its original quality.
- **1/2**: Play your video at half the original size.
- **1/4**: Play your video at a quarter of its original size.

Note: Lowering the playback resolution only affects the preview during editing. It won't change the quality when you export your final video.

Preview Rendering in Filmora

Preview rendering helps make editing smoother by reducing lag, especially when working on complex or high-resolution projects. Filmora lets you choose between two ways to render your video:

1. **Manual Rendering**: You can start the rendering process yourself to improve playback.

2. **Automatic Rendering**: Filmora will automatically render parts of your video as needed, so you don't have to worry about it.

Manual Rendering (By Hand):

When you see the red line appear on your timeline, simply click the "Render" button to start rendering. This is similar to how you add media or make other changes to your timeline. It helps improve playback performance by rendering specific sections of your project.

Once you start rendering, a preview window will appear showing the progress of the render and how much time is left until it's finished.

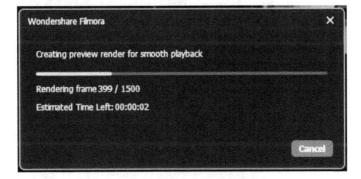

Once the rendering is complete, the red line will turn green, indicating that the preview is fully rendered and ready for smooth playback.

Note: You won't be able to continue editing until the rendering process is complete.

Filmora Auto-Rendering:

Instead of manually clicking the Render button, you can enable Background Render for automatic rendering. This feature automatically renders your videos when you add them to the timeline for editing.

To enable it:

1. Go to File > Preferences > Performance.
2. Turn on Background Render and set a start time.
3. The timeline will begin rendering automatically after five seconds of inactivity.
4. Once done, click OK to save the settings.

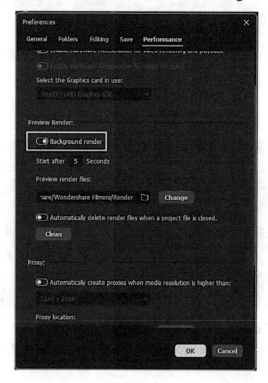

Note: When your timeline is rendered, a green line will appear. If there are any unrendered sections, the line will be red. After making adjustments, updates, or adding effects to the rendered sections, the line will turn red again, signaling that you need to render it once more.

Managing the Timeline and Tracks

The timeline is where you make most of your changes to clips. This guide will help you add, edit, lock, and hide audio and video tracks in Filmora's timeline.

- **Using the Timeline**

The Playhead lets you navigate through the clips you've added to the timeline. It shows you your current position in the video, and the frame where the Playhead is will be displayed in the Preview window.

- **Adjusting the Timeline View**

To adjust the timeline view, hover your mouse over the time section of the timeline. The cursor will change to a two-way arrow. Hold down the left mouse button and drag left or right to zoom in or out on the timeline.

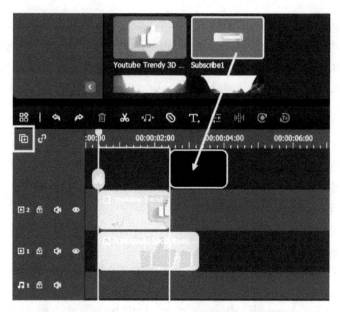

In the top right corner of the timeline, you'll see the Zoom to Fit the Timeline icon. Clicking this will let you see all the media you've added to the timeline. You can also use the zoom slider to adjust the zoom level yourself.

Working with Tracks: Adding, Organizing, and Editing

"Track" means the part of the timeline where your media is placed. In Filmora, you can put video and audio files in tracks, but it's important to remember that videos and audio cannot be placed in the same track.

Adding Track in Filmora:

When you drag something into the timeline, Filmora will automatically make a new track for it. You can add an audio or video file by simply dragging and dropping it into a space on the timeline. You can also click the "Manage Track" button to add, delete, or change any of the tracks.

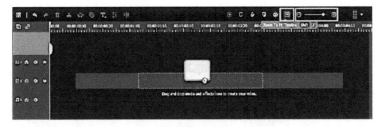

Add Two or More Tracks at the Same Time:

- When you click the Manage Tracks button at the top left corner of the panel, a drop-down menu will appear. This menu lets you add new audio and video tracks or remove the ones you don't need.

- If you click on Open Track Manager, a window will pop up where you can add up to 99 audio and video tracks to your project. You can also use the Placement drop-down menu to choose how the tracks should be arranged on the timeline.

Once you've added new tracks, take a look at them in your timeline to see where they've been placed.

How to Use the Right-Click Menu for Track Options:

To open the options for each track, right-click on the part of the timeline that shows track details (just below the Manage Tracks button).

From there, you can choose Adjust Track Height to make the tracks bigger or smaller based on what you prefer.

Hiding and Locking Tracks on the Timeline

If you want to make something on the track invisible, like a video or a picture, you can do that by clicking on the icon that looks like an eye. This icon is called the Toggle Track Output icon. When you click it, the media on that track will not be shown in the preview or the final video until you turn it back on.

For audio tracks, there is a similar icon that looks like a speaker. This icon is also called the Toggle Track Output icon, and it is used to mute the entire audio track. That means you won't hear any sound from that track while editing or during playback unless you click the icon again to turn the sound back on.

Using the Marker Icon

The Add Marker icon in Filmora is a handy tool that allows you to pinpoint key areas in your video, making the editing process more efficient. By marking important spots on the timeline, you can easily revisit those sections later. This is especially helpful when working on larger projects as it helps keep everything organized and speeds up the editing process.

To use the Add Marker icon, just click on it. It's located in the top right corner of the timeline. When you click it, a marker will appear at the exact position of the playhead, which shows your current location in the video. This lets you quickly return to that spot whenever necessary during your editing.

If you double-click on the marker that you created, the Marker Editor window will open. In this window, you can change the name of the marker, adjust its color, and also add a note or remark.

To put a marker on a video clip, just select it and click the Add Marker button. Taking notes helps you organize your media files better, especially for big projects.

How to Mark Favorites

Users of Wondershare Filmora can already mark their favorite stickers, themes, and effects. However, with the latest update, they can now do much more than just add photos to their favorites, as the system has been greatly improved.

1. Click the Marked Favorites

In the left-hand section of the tab you're using, open up the "Mine" category. Then, pick "Favorites" from the list. Finally, hover your cursor over one of the favorites that appear.

2. Tag Your Favorite Items

After that, right-click on your favorite and select "Add Tag" from the menu. Several options will pop up. You can use the "Commonly Used" and "Recently Used" tags to categorize your favorites, and these categories will appear at the top of your list.

3. Customizing a Tag

If you want to create your tag, just click on "New Tag." A box will pop up where you can type in whatever name you want for it. After typing the name, hit "OK." Your new tag will then show up at the top of the favorites section with the rest of your tags. If you want to add another one later, just click the "+" button below.

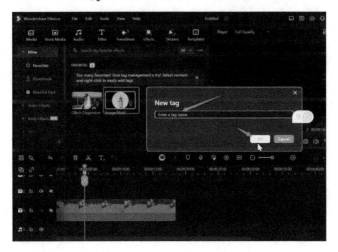

4. Deleting or Removing a Tag

If you don't like a tag or want to change its name, click on "Manage Tag." A small window will pop up showing all your tags. Find the one you want to change, then click the three dots next to it. From there, you can either rename the tag or delete it.

This helps you keep things organized and lets you easily manage the favorites you've marked.

One of the best ways to get better with Filmora is to get familiar with how everything looks and works on the screen. You've already come a long way exploring the Filmora interface, and now you're ready to move on to more helpful guides.

CHAPTER 4

TIPS TO CRAFTING IMPRESSIVE PROJECTS USING FILMORA

Welcome to the Project Creation Section! In this part, we'll be guided through every step of making a project. Whether you're starting a new one or picking up from where you left off, we'll cover everything you need.

You'll learn how to use tools like Instant Mode and Component Templates to save time, and how to use the Filmora Startup Window to create new projects. We'll also show you how to keep your projects organized by opening, moving, and relocating them.

Get ready to dive in and bring your ideas to life with Filmora!

To start a new project in Filmora, you can use either the Startup Window or the Menu Bar. The Startup Window offers a quick and easy way to begin, while the Menu Bar gives you more control. Simply go to the "File" option in the Menu Bar, select "New Project," and you'll be ready to start working on your project. Both methods are simple and efficient for getting your project off the ground.

Exploring the New Startup Window

Take a look at the newly introduced Startup Window. It's designed to be simpler and more informative, helping you understand how Filmora works and how it can assist in creating great videos. The updated window is much easier to navigate and offers helpful insights. You can select the feature you need by clicking on the appropriate tab based on your project goals. Before we start with the editing techniques, let's briefly explore how to make the most of these tools.

Filmora Startup Windows

Note: Update to the most recent version of Filmora if the Startup Window is not visible. After updating, select the General tab under File > Preferences and turn it on. The next time you launch Filmora, the Startup Window will show up.

Creating New Project:

The Create Project page offers a variety of features to help you get started. A feature that allows you to view your work in a variety of ways is the ability to switch between list and thumbnail views for your most recent local projects. With all the resources you require for video production, the new Start-Up Window makes it simple to get started on your project right away. After deciding on your video's aspect ratio, all you need to do is click Create Project to get started.

1. Choose an aspect ratio using the drop-down menu. You can select from a large number of different aspect ratios by selecting the relevant option from this drop-down box.
2. Click New Project to open the new user interface and start editing.

Filmora Startup Windows

Creating a New Project Through the Menu Bar

After Filmora has completely loaded and the interface is visible, you can begin a new project by using the menu bar at the top. To get started, open Filmora and select New Project. This will take you straight to the editing screen where you can begin working on your video. If you'd like to adjust the project settings before you start editing, go to the top menu click on File, then select Project Settings. Here, you can make changes to the resolution of your video, choose your preferred aspect ratio (like widescreen or square), and set the frame rate that works best for your project. These options allow you to tailor your project to meet your exact needs right from the beginning.

Note: If you want to make videos for Instagram, YouTube Shorts, or other social media platforms, you can change the aspect ratio from the default 16:9 to 1:1 (square) or 9:16 (vertical). If you need something different, you can also choose the Custom option to set your aspect ratio.

Saving Your Project in Filmora

In this section, we'll walk you through the steps you need to take to save your project in Filmora. Whether you're storing a project for the first time or want to keep your work up to date, these steps will help you ensure that your creative endeavors are always safe and accessible. You can return to your work later for further editing, sharing, or completion if you save it properly.

1. Click on the 'File' menu located at the top left corner of your screen.

2. Choose 'Save Project' or simply press Ctrl + S to quickly save your work.

3. If you're saving your project for the first time, it's best to use the "Save Project As" option. This allows you to choose a specific location on your computer where the project will be stored. Once you've selected the location, be sure to give your project a clear and descriptive name so it's easy to identify later.

Remember, Filmora will save your project as a .wfp file, allowing you to edit it in the future. Even though Filmora has an auto-save feature, it's always a good idea to save manually too!

Different Ways to Access Your Project in Filmora

This part shows you how to open a project in Filmora so you can continue editing or reviewing your finished work. Whether you're switching between multiple projects or returning to one you worked on earlier, knowing how to open your saved projects helps you stay organized and work smoothly. Here are the steps to get your project back and continue from where you stopped:

1. Open a project from the Startup Window.

2. Go to File > Open Project from the menu bar.

3. Double-click the saved project file on your computer.

1: How to Open a Project in Filmora from the Start-Up Window

1. After launching Filmora, you'll be taken to the Startup Window.

2. Click on 'Open Project' or simply press Ctrl + O to open your file.

3. Browse through your computer to find the saved .wfp project file.

4. Once you find it, click 'Open' to load the project.

5. When the project loads, you'll be able to pick up right where you left off and continue editing.

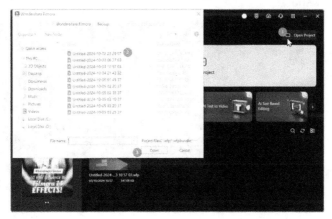

This straightforward method makes it easy for you to manage and access your saved projects whenever you need to.

2: Accessing an Existing Project in the Editing Panel

If you're already working on a project, you can easily open an existing one. Just click on File > Open Recent or File > Open Project to locate your saved .wfp file. You can also use the shortcut Ctrl+O to open it quickly.

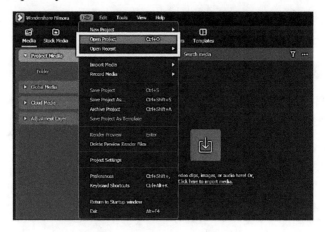

3: Accessing a Project from Filmora Cloud

If you've saved your project to the Filmora Cloud, you can easily access it from the Startup Window in Wondershare Filmora Workspace.

Moving Your Projects in Filmora

Filmora makes it easy to transfer your projects to different storage devices or computers. Whether you're looking to back up your work, free up space, or work on your project from another device, moving your project is simple.

To move your project, open it up, go to File > Archive Project, or use the shortcut Shift + Ctrl + A. This will save your project and all its source files in an archive (.wfp) file, making it easy to pick up where you left off on another computer.

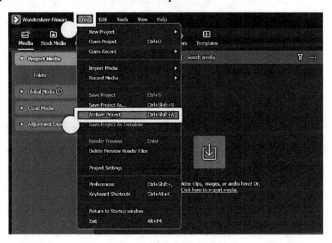

Note: Don't just move the stored project to another computer directly. First, you need to archive the project by selecting File > Archive Project. This ensures that all project files are properly saved and can be accessed on the new device.

Here's a simple way to move your projects in Filmora:

1. Find Your Project Files: Filmora stores all your media files (audio, video, etc.) in a folder and creates a .wfp file for your project. Make sure you know where these files are saved on your computer.
2. Use the Archive Project Option: The Archive Project option in Filmora helps keep everything together by collecting all

relevant media and your project file into one folder. To do this, just click File > Archive Project.

3. **Move the Archived Folder:** Once you've archived the project, you can transfer the entire folder to a new location on your computer, an external hard drive, or cloud storage.

4. **Transfer to Another Computer:** After transferring the folder, open Filmora on the new computer. Select File > Open Project and find the .wfp file to continue editing.

5. **Fix Missing Files (if needed):** If Filmora can't locate certain files, click Locate and direct Filmora to the new location of those files.

This method keeps your projects organized, easy to back up, and portable to other devices.

Relocating Your Filmora Projects

If you move, rename, delete, or detach the external disk where your source files are stored, Filmora will no longer be able to access those files from the saved location. To move projects in Filmora after files have been changed or relocated, follow these steps:

1. If you click on the modified save location or delete the project file, a message will pop up saying that the project can no longer be found in the stored location.

2: If you click on a relocated or missing project file, a "Locate Missing Files" window will appear. It will notify you with a message

saying, "Some file(s) in your project have been moved or are missing." You'll be prompted to select and move the files one by one from the list shown.

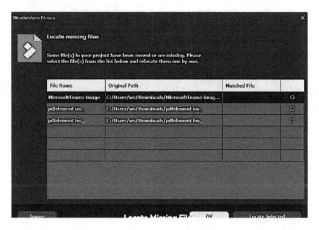

- Choose "Ignore" or "OK." Once you do this, a red exclamation mark will appear in the player interface as soon as the video reaches that point.

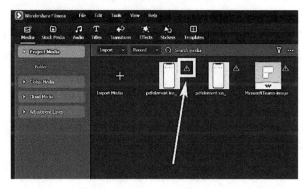

- When you click Locate Selected, a popup will appear showing the source file's save location for project file storage. From there, you can move the missing files to the correct location.

3: If you click on a clip with a red exclamation mark, a message will pop up saying "Unable to locate the file." You can choose from the following options:

- Ignore: This will close the message and return you to the player panel.
- Delete: This will ask you if you're sure you want to delete the clip. Confirm to delete it.
- Relocate: This will open a window where you can find and move the missing files back to the correct location.

Note: If the deleted files are permanently gone, you can select new files to replace them.

CHAPTER 5

IMPORTING, AND RECORDING MEDIA ELEMENTS

In this part, we'll show you simple and smart ways to bring your videos, music, and pictures into Filmora—and how to record your content, too. When you know how to do this well, editing becomes a lot easier and more fun. It also helps you stay organized and get great results faster.

Whether you're making a short video or working on a big project, these tips will help you keep everything in order and focus more on being creative. By the end, you'll know exactly how to add and record media in Filmora without stress.

Smart Tips for Bringing Media into Filmora

1. **Keep Your Files Organized:** Before importing anything, sort your media into folders—like one for videos, another for music, and one for photos. It'll save you time and make editing way smoother.

2. **Stick to Compatible File Types:** Use media formats that Filmora supports. For example, MP4 and MOV for videos, or MP3 and WAV for audio. This helps avoid loading or playback problems later on.

3. **Import Multiple Files at Once:** Instead of dragging files in one by one, select and import a bunch at the same time. It's faster and keeps your workflow on track.

4. **Use the Media Library Wisely:** Learn how to make the most of Filmora's Media Library. It lets you preview, organize, and manage all your files easily in one place.

5. **Check File Quality First:** Make sure your videos, images, and audio are clear and high-quality before you import them. This will help your final video look more professional.

6. **Name Your Files Clearly:** Give your files clear and simple names—like "Intro_Music.mp3" or "Beach_Scene.mp4." This makes it much easier to find the right clip or sound while you're editing, saving you time and effort.
7. **Always Back Up Your Media:** To stay safe, keep a backup of your media on an external hard drive or in the cloud. That way, if something goes wrong, you won't lose your files.

Instructions For Setting Up Imported Media In Filmora

- To classify material (music, video clips, and photos), use folders.
- To make identification easier, rename media with descriptive titles.
- Use tags to group media according to projects or themes.
- Create a standard naming scheme (such as "ProjectName_Date_Description").
- Examine and arrange media according to kind, date added, or duration.
- To lessen clutter, remove unnecessary media regularly.
- To avoid data loss, make an external backup of your arranged folders.

How to Organize Your Imported Media in Filmora

Keep your editing smooth and stress-free by setting up your imported media the right way. Here are some easy tips to help you stay organized:

- **Use folders** to sort your files into categories like music, video clips, and photos.
- **Rename your files** with clear, descriptive names so you know exactly what each one is at a glance.
- **Add tags** to group media by project or theme—this makes everything easier to find later.

74

- **Stick to a naming system**, like "ProjectName_Date_Description," to keep everything consistent.
- **Sort your media** by type, when it was added, or how long it is to keep things tidy.
- **Delete media you don't need** anymore to reduce clutter.
- **Always back up** your organized folders to an external drive or cloud storage so you don't lose anything important.

With a little setup, you'll save time and avoid frustration every time you edit.

Importing Media into Filmora

Filmora lets you easily import videos, music, and photos in HD, 4K, or standard quality. Once imported, all your files appear in the Media Library, ready to use in your project. You can import files in several ways. First, you can choose to import individual media files, which is perfect for adding a single video, audio track, or image. If you have a whole folder of related files, it's best to use the "Import a Media Folder" option—this keeps everything together and organized. You can also import media straight from your camera or phone if that's where your content is stored. Lastly, for quick trimming without losing video quality, use the "Import with Instant Cutter Tool." This is especially helpful for simple edits when you don't need to go through the full timeline.

2. Click on the **Import Media** section to open a pop-up box, then choose one or more media files you want to add to your project.

3. You can also drag and drop your media files directly into the workspace. This makes importing quick and easy and helps you stay organized while working on your project.

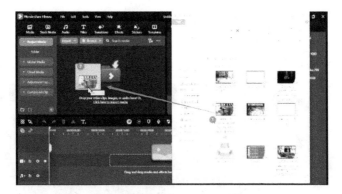

To make your editing faster, Filmora may prompt you to create a proxy file when importing media. A proxy file is a smaller version of your original media, making it easier to work with, especially for high-definition videos. Using proxy files improves timeline performance without affecting the quality of your final export. It's a good idea to select "Yes" to generate proxy files and streamline your editing process.

How to Select Multiple Files at Once

To select several files at the same time:

- **Use the Ctrl key**: Hold down the Ctrl key and click on each file you want. This is great if the files are not next to each other in the list.
- **Use the Shift key**: Click on the first file, then hold down Shift and click on the last file in the group. This selects all the files between them.

Keep holding Ctrl or Shift while you click. Once you're done, just release the key—your selected files will stay highlighted and ready to import or move.

Recording and Capturing Media Files in Filmora

Filmora lets you easily record content right from your computer. Whether you want to capture your screen, record yourself using a webcam, or add a voiceover, Filmora has simple tools to help. In this section, we'll walk through three key features:

- Recording webcam footage directly in Filmora

- Capturing your PC screen

- Recording voiceovers for your videos

These tools are great for tutorials, reaction videos, online classes, or personal projects.

Recording a Webcam Video in Filmora (Made Easy)

1. Before you start, just check that your webcam is properly connected to your computer.
2. Then, open Filmora and look for the **Record** button at the top-left corner of the Media Library. Click it, and you're on your way to recording with your webcam!

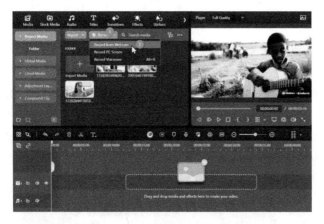

3. When the Capture Video box opens, click the camera icon to start recording. Click the same icon again when you're done to stop.

4. Once you stop recording, click OK to save the video to the Captured Files folder.

5. The video will automatically appear in your Media Library right after it's recorded.

6. To find the video on your computer, right-click on it in the Media Library and choose Reveal in Explorer.

7. If you want to start editing, just drag the video onto your Timeline.

Record Your Computer Screen

To record your screen, go to the Record menu and choose Record PC Screen. This opens the Filmora Screen Recorder window. Here, you can select which part of the screen you want to capture and set the video size. When you're ready, click the red record button to start. Press F9 on your keyboard to stop the recording. Once it's done, the video will automatically appear in your Media Library, so you can easily drag it into your timeline for editing.

Record a Voiceover

Before you start, make sure your microphone is properly plugged into your computer. Then, go to the Record menu and choose Record Voiceover. When you click the microphone button, you'll get a 3-second countdown before recording begins. As you speak, your voice will be recorded and added directly to the timeline as an audio track.

Import Files from Cloud Storage in Filmora

1. Click the Import button at the top left of the screen.
2. From the dropdown menu, select Import from Cloud.
3. Choose the cloud service you'd like to use—such as Google Drive, Dropbox, or OneDrive.
4. If prompted, sign in to your cloud account.
5. Browse and select the media files you want to bring into Filmora.
6. Click Import, and the files will appear in your Media Library.
7. You can now rename, tag, or sort the files into folders to keep everything organized.

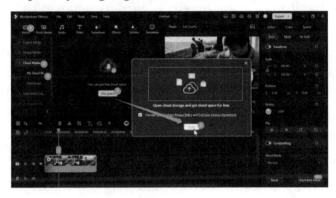

Exporting Your Video in Filmora

Exporting is the final and most important step in your video editing journey with Filmora. After spending time editing your clips, adding transitions, and effects, and syncing audio, this step turns your project into a video file that you can save, share, or burn onto a DVD.

Filmora makes exporting easy and flexible. Whether you're sharing on YouTube, posting on social media, or preparing a business presentation, you can choose the best quality settings for your needs. You'll find simple options to adjust the resolution, frame rate, and bitrate—even if you're not a tech expert.

With Filmora's clear and user-friendly interface, you'll be able to export your video in just a few clicks—ready to share with the world.

Key Export Settings for Filmora Files

When you're ready to export your video in Filmora, start by picking the right file format for your project. MP4 is great for online use, MOV works well for high-quality editing, and MP3 is perfect if you're just exporting audio. Depending on where you'll be sharing your video, you can choose a resolution: go for 4K if you want ultra-high definition, 1080p for YouTube, or 720p and 480p for smaller files that upload faster.

For frame rates, you can select 24 fps for a movie-style look, 30 fps for regular online videos, or 60 fps for super smooth motion. The bitrate controls both the quality and the file size: higher means better quality but a bigger file, while a lower bitrate keeps the file smaller at the cost of some quality. For the best compression, H.264 keeps your file small without losing too much quality, while H.265 is better if you're working with 4K videos.

Filmora also lets you tweak audio settings, offering different sample rates and bitrates for better sound. You can choose stereo or mono depending on your needs. In terms of video quality, you can choose "Best" for the highest quality or "Good" for smaller files with lower quality. If you're sharing on social media, you can pick the right aspect ratio, like 16:9 for widescreen or 1:1 for square videos.

Lastly, enabling GPU Acceleration can speed up your export process, and Filmora makes it easy to share your video directly to platforms like YouTube, Instagram, or TikTok.

Knowing these options helps you tailor the export process to fit your project, whether you're aiming for high-quality production or content that's easy to upload and share.

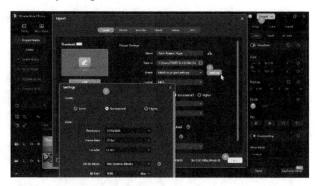

Organizing Media Files in Filmora

Keeping your media files well-organized in Filmora is key to maintaining an efficient workflow and ensuring your projects remain tidy and easy to navigate. Here's how to organize your media library:

1. Set up folders for different media types. Use Filmora's folder feature to group items like audio tracks, images, and video clips. This helps you stay organized and access everything with ease.

2. Once you've imported your media, give your files unique names. Change generic filenames like "IMG_001" to

something more descriptive, such as "Interview_Clip_1" or "Background Music," so you can quickly identify them during editing.

3. Organize your media by audio, video, or image. You can also sort your files by Title, Length, Category, or Creation Date. Choose whether you want to view your files in ascending or descending order, and sort them by Name, Duration, Type, or Date Created. This is where you can filter your media based on file type.

CHAPTER 6

ESSENTIAL FILMORA EDITING TECHNIQUES

This chapter covers the basic editing techniques that will take your videos to the next level. Learn how to apply advanced effects like motion tracking, chroma key, picture-in-picture, and split-screen, along with essential video edits such as cropping, panning, zooming, splitting, and trimming. For audio, you'll dive into adding effects, fading, and pitch adjustments. You'll also explore tools like color correction, stabilization, and speed adjustments, giving you everything you need to produce professional-quality videos.

Transferring Media Clips to the Filmora Timeline

Before you can start editing your video, you need to bring your media clips into Filmora's timeline, where all the action happens. This section will guide you through the simple yet essential process of moving your clips from the media library to the timeline, where you'll begin crafting your project.

Whether you're working with video footage, images, or audio, understanding how to organize and place your clips on the timeline is the first step toward creating a polished final product. With Filmora's intuitive interface, you'll be able to easily drag and drop your media, setting the foundation for all your creative edits.

Let's get started and lay the groundwork for your video masterpiece!

1. Open the Media Library and import your media files.
2. Select the audio, video, or image file from the Media Library.
3. Drag the selected media file onto the timeline.
4. Position the clip on the timeline where you'd like it.
5. Adjust the timeline layers for effects, audio, or video as needed.

85

Cropping, Panning, and Zooming in Your Video

Cropping lets you trim your video to a particular aspect ratio, ensuring that only the chosen area is shown when the video is played. You can also use the Pan & Zoom effect to simulate camera movements, like zooming in or out. For instance, you might begin with a wide shot and then gradually zoom in to highlight a specific subject, followed by a pan to uncover other details or subjects in the scene. This technique adds dynamic movement to your video, making it more engaging.

To make it happen, follow these steps:

1. Select the video clip on the timeline.
2. Right-click the clip and choose "Crop and Zoom" from the menu that appears.

3. A Crop and Zoom box will pop up, allowing you to choose the next action. The task is shown below.

4. For the same outcome, you can also click the crop icon located above the timeline. Once you select the video clip from the timeline, the icon will appear automatically.

5. Use the corner handles inside the square to resize and reposition the crop area.

Click "Apply" to confirm and apply the crop to the video.

How to Split and Trim Media Clips

You can easily cut or split video clips to remove parts you don't need. This way, you can break a video into two separate clips, or trim the start and/or end. Splitting or trimming the clip won't affect the original file.

Steps to Split a Video in Filmora:

Here's how to split a video clip:

1. Add your video to the timeline.
2. Move the playhead to the spot where you want to split the video.
3. Click the Scissors (Split) icon or right-click and choose "Split."
4. Repeat the process to split the video at other points as needed.
5. Edit, rearrange, or remove the sections you've split.

Note: If you don't select a track, all the clips under the playhead will be split. To split just one track, first select the track, then click the Split button. If you can't see the Split button, go to File -> Preferences -> Editing and make sure it's enabled.

How to Use Quick Split Mode

1. Click the pointer icon found just above the timeline on the left.

2. Choose **Quick Split Mode** from the dropdown menu.

3. While reviewing your video, use Quick Split to make fast, simple cuts as you go.

Trimming Clips with the Trim Media Tool

You can easily cut out unwanted sections from the beginning or end of a video using the trim tool.

1: Trim Using Mark In & Mark Out in the Preview Window:

You can trim your video even before adding it to the timeline by setting start and end points in the Preview window.

1. Double-click the video in the Media Library to open it in the Preview window.

2. Find the point where you want the clip to begin and click the Mark In button.

3. Move to where you want the clip to end and click the Mark Out button.

4. Drag the trimmed portion from the Preview window onto the timeline to include it in your project.

Note: Once you've set the Mark In and Mark Out points, you can still adjust them by dragging the markers to new spots within the Preview window. However, you won't be able to insert the same trimmed clip into the timeline again—you'll need to drag it over once more if you want to use it.

2: Trimming Directly from the Timeline

Choose the video clip you want to edit on the timeline. Hover your mouse over the left or right edge of the clip until the trim icon appears. Then, click and drag the edge inward or outward to remove the parts you don't need.

Filmora also offers the ability to quickly cut a clip from the start or finish. To trim the playhead, place it on the chosen frame and then use the Trim Start to Playhead or Trim End to Playhead options from the Trim context menu to trim everything in front of or behind the playhead.

Making the Most of Motion Tracking in Filmora

Motion tracking in Filmora is a super useful feature that lets you follow the movement of any object in your video. You can easily attach things like text, images, or effects to a moving person or item—perfect for making your videos more eye-catching and professional. Whether you're spotlighting a player in a sports clip, adding a fun label to someone in your vlog, or making social media content pop, motion tracking helps you bring your ideas to life.

With Filmora's Motion Tracker tool, you can track how something moves and have your text or images follow along. While this kind of editing usually requires fancy equipment and software, Filmora makes it simple. You can even save the motion path as a template, tweak it later, or replace certain parts with your graphics. It's a creative, easy way to add personality and polish to your videos.

Practical Uses of Motion Tracking in Video Editing and Film

- Motion tracking helps you stick to text, images, or graphics of people or objects as they move—keeping everything aligned smoothly.
- Use it to make effects like explosions, lighting, or animations move in sync with the scene.
- Easily swap out items in a scene, like changing what's in someone's hand or updating content on a moving screen.
- Make titles and captions that follow characters or objects, adding flair and clarity.
- Use motion tracking to automatically blur faces, license plates, or other private info that moves through a scene.
- Draw attention to important parts of your story using tracked arrows, highlights, or icons.
- Seamlessly blend augmented reality graphics into live footage for a futuristic, immersive look.
- Track players, balls, or vehicles in sports footage to display real-time stats or insights.
- Useful for applying filters, effects, or animations based on body or facial movement.
- Improve video quality by using tracking data to stabilize unsteady camera movements.

How to Track Movement in a Video Clip

1. Click on the video clip in your timeline to open the editing options.
2. Head over to the AI Tools section and select the Motion Tracking feature.
3. Drag and position the tracking box over the moving object you want to follow.
4. Click Start Motion Track to begin tracking the motion.

Tip: Make sure the object stays visible in the frame for the entire duration. If it doesn't, try trimming or shortening the clip for better results.

Motion tracking is a great way to keep an eye on how your subject moves or changes throughout the video.

Adding the Tracking Object and Making Adjustments

1. Pick what you want to add—this could be text, an image, a graphic, or even another video clip.
2. Drag and drop your chosen element onto the track above your main video.
3. Move the element around until it's exactly where you want it to start on the screen.
4. Adjust the size and alignment of the element so it fits naturally with the video.
5. Make sure the added element follows the movement of the tracked object to keep everything looking smooth and in sync.

6. Play it back, fine-tune it if needed, and make sure everything feels seamless and professional.

Attach an Object to Follow the Motion

First, select the video clip that has motion tracking applied to your timeline. Then, under the Motion Tracking options, click on Link Element. Choose the object you want—such as text, an image, or a graphic—and it will automatically follow the tracked movement in your video.

If a confirmation message appears, simply click OK to apply the motion tracking effect. After that, go ahead and select the element you want to link—like text, an image, or another asset—to follow the tracked movement.

Preview and Adjust the Tracking Result

Once the tracking is complete, play back the video to see how everything moves. In the preview window, you can fine-tune the linked object by adjusting its size and position as needed. If you'd like, you can also switch out the linked element at any time for a different one.

Disable or Remove Motion Tracking

To turn off motion tracking, click on your video clip and go to the Video tab. From there, open the AI Tools menu and simply uncheck the Motion Tracking option. This will remove the effect from your clip.

Creative Uses for Motion Tracking in Filmora

1. **Censoring Objects:** If you need to hide something for privacy or copyright reasons, Filmora lets you blur or place icons over objects that move along with them throughout the video.

2. **Enhancing Real Estate Videos:** Motion tracking can make property videos more dynamic. You can add tags and prices that follow the property, highlight key features, guide viewers with arrows, and blur sensitive areas like faces or unfinished rooms for a polished finish.

3. **Adding Motion-Tracked Text:** Make your videos more engaging by attaching text or logos that follow objects in the scene. You can also add motion-tracked captions for key points or show a character's thoughts or speech creatively.

Tip: If the motion tracking window isn't showing up, update Filmora and go to File > Preferences > General to enable it. It will appear the next time you open the program.

Using The Filmora Chroma Key and The Green Screen Tools

A tool called Chroma Key is used to remove specific colors from pictures or videos. For instance, Chroma Key can eliminate green spots while filming a subject in front of a green screen or when a portion of the subject is covered in green. This enables you to create thrilling effects, such as a superhero flying through the skies, by inserting the subject into various virtual settings.

Creative Uses of Chroma Key in Video Editing

Chroma Key in video editing goes beyond just removing backgrounds. It's a powerful tool with many creative uses:

1. **Take Characters to Imaginary Settings**: Instead of real backgrounds, you can replace the green screen with beautiful images to transport characters to any place—whether historical, fantasy, or outer space.

2. **Create Animated Visual Effects**: You can make eye-catching effects like characters flying or teleporting by layering them over moving backgrounds, such as futuristic cityscapes.

3. **Interactive Tutorials and Presentations**: Use Chroma Key to blend charts, images, or live websites into video presentations. This is great for business presentations or instructional videos where you interact with content in real time.

4. **Combine Multiple Characters**: Record different characters separately and then merge them into one scene using Chroma Key. This works well for mixing animated characters with live-action footage.

5. **Add Animated Elements**: Chroma Key allows you to insert animated objects, text, and motion graphics seamlessly into your videos. Think of pop-up visuals or interactive titles that fit naturally into your scenes.

6. **Enhance Virtual Tours and Real Estate Videos**: Highlight specific features of a property during virtual tours by overlaying text, arrows, or markers. This helps guide viewers through different rooms interactively.

7. **Simulate Weather Effects**: You can mimic weather conditions like rain or snow without filming outdoors. By layering weather videos, you can control the look of any scene.

8. **Create Smooth Transitions**: Use the Chroma Key to transition smoothly between scenes. For example, film someone approaching the camera on a green screen, then move them to a different location seamlessly.

9. **Blend Different Media**: Combine drawings, animations, or other media with live-action video using Chroma Key. This mix creates unique and captivating videos that blend various artistic styles.

Applying Chroma Key to Your Video

Using Chroma Key in Filmora is an easy process. Follow these steps to make the most of the feature:

1. **Prepare Your Clips**:

Ensure that the main video is filmed with a green screen or solid color backdrop. Then, open Filmora and import both your main video (the one with the green screen) and the background video or image you want to use.

2. **Add Videos to the Timeline**:

Place the background video or image on the bottom track (Video Track 1) of the timeline. This sets the foundation for the Chroma Key effect to blend your green-screen footage with the new background seamlessly.

Drag the green screen clip onto the timeline, above the backdrop clip (Video Track 2). To adjust it, move the handle as shown below.

3. Enable the Chroma Key tool:

Double-click the green screen clip and go to the Ai Tools Tab to turn on the Chroma Key option. The green screen color will be selected and removed automatically. You can adjust the offset, tolerance, edge thickness, and edge feather settings to improve the quality of the background video.

To make the green screen overlay blend smoothly with the background, adjust the settings in the Compositing tab.

4. Adjust Tolerance:

- To get the perfect effect, tweak the tolerance settings. This controls how closely the selected color matches the colors in the clip. A higher tolerance removes more shades of that color.

- Using the "Edge Feather" option can help soften the edges, making the blend with the background look smoother.

5. Preview to see the Changes:

Check the preview window to see how well the Chroma Key effect is working. If needed, make further adjustments.

6. Finalize and Export:

Enhance your video by adding titles, motion graphics, or other effects if desired. Once you're satisfied with the result, click "Export" to save your video in the format you prefer.

Tips for Best Results:

1. Use even lighting to avoid shadows on the green screen.
2. Keep the subject distant from the green screen to reduce color spill.
3. Use a high-quality camera for clearer footage and better Chroma Key results.

Using Mask Effects in Your Video

Masking creates a transparent layer that you place over the main clip. Only the section covered by the mask will be visible, while the rest is hidden. This technique is mainly used to highlight a specific subject or action, directing the viewer's focus and reducing distractions.

How to Apply a Mask in Filmora:

1. **Import Your Movie:** Open Filmora, then drag and drop your video onto the timeline.
2. **Access the Masking Tool:** Select the video on the timeline, click on the "Mask" option under the Video tab, and choose a shape that suits your project.
3. **Customize the Mask:** Adjust the mask's size, shape, feathering, rotation, and position using the settings in the Mask section.

4. **Preview and Export the video:** Check the video to ensure the mask looks right, then go ahead and export your final version.

Feel free to choose any shape you'd like. Let's try applying a heart shape by following the same steps as before.

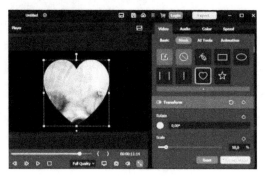

This technique enhances your visual storytelling by allowing you to control what's shown and what's hidden, giving you more creative freedom.

Sketching and Customizing with the Masking Tool

The Draw Mask feature simplifies creating detailed masks. By dragging control points and working with B-Splines, you can design intricate shapes and customize them exactly how you want."

"To draw the mask accurately, you'll need to zoom in and out of the player screen. For smooth curves, simply modify the Bessel curve of the drawn mask by holding down the Alt/Option key. Additionally, you can save your draw mask as a preset, allowing you to apply it with just one click whenever needed."

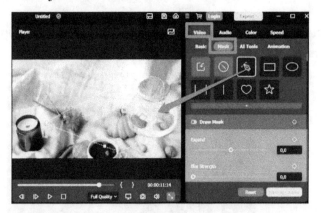

In the preview window, you can use the handles to resize, move, or rotate the mask as needed. For more precise adjustments, the sliders on the Mask tab give you the flexibility to fine-tune settings like width, height, radius, blur strength, rotation, scale, and location. You can even flip the mask to hide the previously visible area and reveal the opposite side.

Adding Keyframes in Masking

Keyframes are crucial in animation and film, marking the beginning and end of a smooth transition. They're called "frames" because they represent specific moments in time, whether on a film strip or within a digital video editing timeline.

Here's how to add keyframes:

1. To set your first keyframe, move the playhead to the spot you want, select the clip on your timeline, and open the edit menu.

2. To add your second keyframe, just move the playhead to the next point. At this stage, you can adjust the mask by creating animation effects, rotating, resizing, or changing the blur strength.

Keyframe Application in Masking

Keyframes are crucial in animation and film, marking the beginning and end of a smooth transition. They're called "frames" because they represent specific moments in time, whether on a film strip or within a digital video editing timeline.

Here's how to add keyframes:

1. To set your first keyframe, move the playhead to the spot you want, select the clip on your timeline, and open the edit menu.
2. To add your second keyframe, just move the playhead to the next point. At this stage, you can adjust the mask by creating animation effects, rotating, resizing, or changing the blur strength.

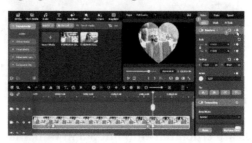

To save your custom mask for later, just click "Store as Custom." If you want to go back to the original settings, click "Reset." To see how the mask looks, click "Play" in the Preview window or press the Spacebar. When you're finished, save your project by pressing Ctrl+S.

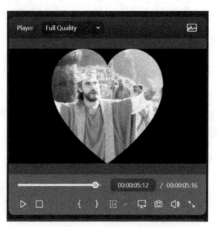

Using the Filmora Text Tool

Filmora's Text Tool makes it easy to add editable text to your videos, like titles, subtitles, captions, and lower thirds. You can quickly adjust the font, size, color, and placement of your text to make it look just right. You can even add effects or animations to make it stand out more. With a wide range of pre-made text styles and motion effects, Filmora helps you create dynamic text for credits, intros, or notes in no time. This versatile tool is perfect for adding clarity and emphasis to your video.

Filmora Text Options for Creative Video Projects

In video editing, clear communication is essential to keep your audience hooked. Filmora helps you tell your story more engagingly with a variety of text options. Whether you're adding fun callouts, informative subtitles, or attention-grabbing headlines, there are endless ways to use text to get your message across. This section takes a closer look at all the different text options Filmora has to offer.

Here are the available text options in Filmora to enhance your projects:

1. **3D Titles**: Text that appears three-dimensional, adding depth and visual impact.

2. **Callouts**: Text with arrows or shapes that highlight specific areas of the screen.

3. **End Credits**: Templates for static or scrolling credits, typically used to list contributors at the end of a video.

4. **Motion Titles**: Text with animated elements that add movement and style to titles.

5. **Openers**: Dynamic and attention-grabbing text templates designed for the opening sequences.

6. **Speech Bubbles**: Comic-style text bubbles, perfect for commentary or comedic content.

7. **Subtitles**: Simplified text used for displaying dialogue, captions, or lower thirds at the bottom of the screen.

8. **Text Backdrops**: Vibrant or patterned backgrounds that enhance text visibility or highlight particular text.

9. **Text Effects**: Special effects like glowing, bouncing, or typewriter-style movements that make text stand out.

10. **Text Masks**: Using text as a mask for images or video clips, allowing visuals to show through while the text is cut out.

11. **Text Overlays**: Decorative text elements with built-in animations, often adding an artistic touch to videos.

12. **Typography Presets**: Creative text layouts with distinctive font combinations, ideal for visual storytelling or social media posts.

13. **Titles**: Pre-made text templates are typically used at the start of a video for introductions.

Additionally, user-created text templates with custom fonts, colors, and animations can be saved for future use.

How to Add Text to Your Projects:

1. Import Your Media: You can either drag your video clips directly into the media library or click the "Import" button to add them to Filmora. Once imported, drag your video clip onto the timeline to start editing.

2. Choose a Text Template: To browse different text templates like Openers, Subtitles, and Credits, click on the "Titles" tab. Select the one that suits your project and drag it onto the timeline above your video clip.

3. **Edit Text Properties:** Just double-click on the text layer to open the text editor. From there, you can easily change the text's content, font, size, color, and position to make it fit perfectly with your video's style.

4. **Add Animations (Optional):** Filmora gives you the option to add animations to your text, adding more movement and style. You can pick from a range of effects, such as motion or fade-ins, to enhance the text's visual impact.

Preview the text by playing the video to see how it looks after editing. You can then adjust the duration, text length, or any other properties to ensure it fits perfectly.

Applying Stickers in Filmora

Stickers are a fun and creative way to add extra style to your Filmora videos. They can help tell your story, evoke emotions, and increase viewer engagement. Here's how to use stickers in Filmora:

1. **Accessing Stickers**: Open your project and go to the "Stickers" section. Click on it and scroll through the various sticker options available.
2. **Selecting Stickers**: Once you've found the sticker you want, simply drag and drop it onto the timeline above your video clip.

3. Adjusting Size and Position: To resize or reposition the sticker, click on it in the preview window and adjust it as needed.

4. Customizing Stickers: Enhance the sticker's visibility by applying animations or effects. You can also adjust its duration on the timeline to match the video.

5. Previewing Changes: Ensure the sticker fits seamlessly into your video by previewing it and making sure it looks just right.

Create a Snapshot from a Video Clip

Still, images from video clips can be great for thumbnails, promotional content, or capturing a specific moment in your video. Filmora makes it simple to take high-quality snapshots directly from your video during the editing process. Here's how:

1. In the timeline, choose the video and play it. Pause at the moment you want to capture.

2. Click the camera icon beneath the preview window to capture the image.

3. The image will be saved as a still in the project library. You can choose the save location and change the file format (JPG, PNG).

To locate the image on your computer, right-click on it in the media library and select "Reveal in Explorer."

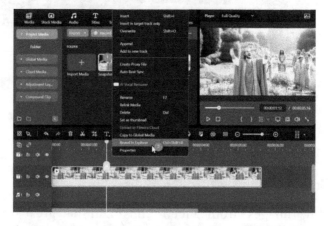

Note: You don't need to pause the video before clicking the camera. The image will automatically be saved as a .png file.

CHAPTER 7

INNOVATIVE TECHNIQUES AND HACKS

In this chapter, you'll learn how to make your videos look and sound even better using some fun and powerful editing tools. We'll show you how to use cool effects like mosaic blur, face-off, and freeze frame. You'll also learn how to create split-screen and picture-in-picture videos, and even how to play your video in reverse.

We'll guide you through improving video quality with color correction, stabilizing shaky footage, and changing the speed of your clips with speed ramping. For sound, you'll learn how to cut audio, change the pitch, and use equalizers to fine-tune the sound. These tools will help you make creative, professional-looking videos.

Using Reverse Speed in Filmora

Reversing a video means playing it backward, and it's a fun way to make your videos more interesting. This effect can help creatively tell your story, highlight important moments, or just add a cool, unexpected twist. You can use it to rewind an action scene, play something in reverse for fun, or give your video a unique look.

How to Apply Reverse Speed in Filmora

You can make your video play backward using the Reverse feature in Wondershare Filmora. Here's how to do it:

Using the Edit Menu:

1. Select the Clip – Import your video and drag the clip you want to reverse into the timeline.

2. Enable Reverse Speed – Double-click the clip to open the editing menu, then check the Reverse Speed option.

3. Preview and Adjust: Watch the reversed video to see how it looks. Adjust the speed until you get the effect you want.

4. Export: Once you're satisfied with the video, save the reversed clip by exporting it.

Using the Speed Tool on the Timeline:

1. Choose the clip on the timeline.
2. Click the Speed Icon (looks like a speedometer) above the timeline toolbar.
3. Select "Reverse" from the dropdown menu.
4. Use the preview window to watch the reversed clip.
5. Adjust the speed if necessary.
6. Export the video.

This easy method can strongly change how your video feels and the message it gives.

Picture-in-Picture (PIP) Effect in Filmora

The Picture-in-Picture (PIP) effect is a popular video technique that allows you to place a smaller video on top of a larger one. This effect is frequently used to display multiple video clips simultaneously on the same screen, making it suitable for various content types.

PIP is particularly beneficial for creating product demonstrations, online tutorials, gaming videos, and other content where an additional video is needed to complement the main footage. For example, you could narrate a game while showing a live camera feed in a smaller window or describe a process shown in the main video. This versatile effect enhances viewer engagement and provides additional context, whether you're offering instructions or commenting on a key film scene.

How to Add a PIP Effect to Your Video

To add a PIP effect to your video, follow these steps:

1. Import Videos: First, bring your smaller PIP video into your media library along with your main background video.
2. Place Background Video in Timeline: Drag your background video into Video Track 1 on the timeline.
3. Position PIP Video Above Background: Drag the PIP video onto a track above the background video in the timeline. This will layer the PIP video over the background video.

4. Now it's time to make the PIP effect by placing the smaller video on top of the background video.

- Click on the PIP video in the timeline. Then, drag the corners in the Preview window to resize and move it where you want.

- You can adjust the PIP clip's shape, and blending style, add a border, or make it any size you like by dragging it around.

- To change the shape of your PIP video, hover over different mask shapes in the Edit panel and pick the one you like.

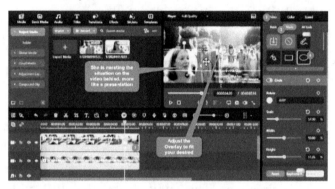

Change the PIP Video's Blending Mode

You can make your PIP video blend in cool ways with the background by changing its blending mode. This adds a more exciting and dynamic look to your video.

1. Select the PIP Video: Click on the PIP video in the timeline. This will open the Video Edit panel. Then, go to the *Basic* tab.
2. Pick a Blend Mode: Scroll down to the *Compositing* section. Choose a blend mode like *Multiply*, *Darken*, *Screen*, or *Color Burn* to create different effects.

3. Adjust the Opacity: Use the *Opacity* slider to make the PIP video more or less see-through until it looks just right in the Preview window.

Add Animation, Motion, and Effects to Your PIP Video in Filmora

You can make your PIP video even more fun by adding motion effects and animations in Filmora.

1. Open the Animation Panel: Double-click the PIP video in the timeline to open the Video Edit panel. Then, switch from the *Basic* tab to the *Animation* tab.

2. Apply Motion or Animation: Find an animation or motion preset you like. Double-click it, or right-click and choose *Apply*. You can watch a preview of the effect in the Preview window to see how it looks.

3. Add Effects to Your PIP Video

You can make your PIP video look even better by adding effects.

- First, click on the PIP video in the timeline.
- If you want, you can drag a border effect onto it.
- Then, go to the *Effect* tab in the Video panel. Browse through the available effects and apply the ones you like to boost your video's visual style.

Change the Look of Your PIP Video

You can easily change the style, color, and other details of your PIP video in Filmora to match your creative vision. Here's how:

1. Open the Video Edit Panel: Click on the PIP video in the timeline to open the edit options.
2. Adjust Colors: Go to the *Color* tab to tweak the hue, saturation, contrast, and brightness.
3. Edit Position and Size: In the *Basic* tab, you can change the position, rotation, and scale of your PIP video.
4. Blend and Opacity: In the *Compositing* section, you can adjust the blend mode and opacity to get the perfect look.

How to Create a Split-Screen Project in Filmora

Filmora's split-screen feature lets you show several videos at once on one screen — perfect for comparison videos, reaction videos, or telling a story from different angles. It's easy to use with Filmora's ready-made templates and can make your videos look much more professional and exciting.

With the split-screen tool, you can replay your story across multiple screens. Use it to show side-by-side comparisons, different viewpoints, or even high-quality gameplay clips. Just follow the steps below to get started!

Choose a Split Screen Preset

Filmora makes it easy to combine multiple videos into a cool split-screen layout. Using simple drag-and-drop tools and advanced editing options, you can creatively tell your story. Just follow these steps to get started:

1. Open Filmora and click on *New Project*. Then, import all the video clips you want to use.
2. Go to the *Templates* section and click on *Split Screen*. You'll find over 86 preset templates! You can add up to six video clips to play together at the same time.

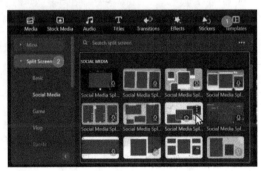

3. Double-click on any of the split-screen thumbnails to preview what the layouts look like. When you find one you like, drag it down to the timeline to use it.

By default, the split-screen lasts five seconds, but you can easily change that. Just drag the edges of the clip in the timeline forward or backward to adjust the length.

Tip: To quickly switch between different template categories like *Basic* and *Social Media*, scroll up and down with your mouse wheel in the thumbnail area. (You'll only need to scroll horizontally.)

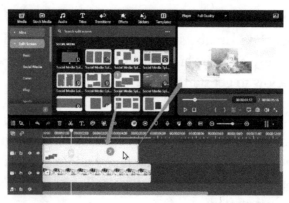

4. Add Your Videos to the Split Screen. Just drag and drop your imported video clips into the spaces provided by the template. Each section will hold one video, and they'll all play together at the same time. Simply drag each video clip into place one by one.

5. Fine-Tune the Split-Screen Video: Editing the color on a split-screen video is just like working on any regular clip. Start by selecting the clip you want to adjust. In the Property

Panel, click on the Color section. Here, you can set the perfect color tone for your scene, adjust the White Balance to make the video look warmer or cooler, and tweak the Light settings to get the right brightness and contrast. You can also use the Color Match tool to keep the colors looking consistent across all your clips and add a Vignette to gently darken the edges of the frame.

You can easily apply the look you want by using the curve tool. Just go to the Color tab, find the Curve, and slide it up or down to make your adjustments, like this:

You can also fine-tune your video and get the look you want using the Color Wheels. Check out the screenshot below to see how it works:

Bring Your Split Screen to Life with Animation

To make your split-screen videos stand out, try adding some animation effects. Just double-click the split screen you're using, then head over to the Animation tab and pick from the available motion presets. You can preview how it looks in the Preview Panel and add the animation to your video once you're happy with it!

You can also add animation to each clip inside your split-screen video. Just open the Advanced Edit window to get started!

Edit Each Video Inside the Split Screen

In Filmora, you can easily tweak each video within a split-screen layout. Just click on the clip you want to edit. You can resize, move, or rotate each video to fit your design. You can also adjust colors, change the opacity, and apply filters to individual clips to make sure everything looks just right. Split-screen editing also gives you plenty of creative options to make your video truly stand out!

- Use the slider on the split-screen preview to zoom in or out of a selected clip.
- You can mute the audio for any single clip if you want.
- To remove a video from the split screen, just select the clip and click the Delete button in the preview box.

With these tools, you have plenty of ways to polish your split-screen video. Just go to Edit and open the Advanced Split Screen window.

Here, you can rotate clips, move or resize them, adjust colors, and even add motion effects to bring your video to life!

How to Use the Drop Shadow Effect in Filmora

The Drop Shadow effect in Filmora is a great way to add depth and make your videos, text, or images pop. It gives your project a more realistic and professional look. Here's how you can easily add a drop shadow to your video:

1: Add Your Video or Image to the Timeline

- First, drag and drop your video or image onto the timeline.
- If you're using a PIP (picture-in-picture) clip, adjust its mask, position, and size as needed.

2: Apply the Drop Shadow Effect

- Click on the clip you want to edit to open the settings.
- In the Property Panel on the right side, go to Video > Basic and look for Drop Shadow.
- Turn on the Drop Shadow by clicking the switch.

  Now your clip will have a stylish shadow effect that adds a professional touch!

3: Preview Your Project to Finish

Once you're done, take a moment to preview your project to make sure everything looks just the way you want it.

Applying the Mosaic Blur Effect to Your Video

The Mosaic Blur effect lets you pixelate specific areas of your video, making it great for hiding things like faces, license plates, or other personal details. It's commonly used to protect privacy in videos. Here's how to use it:

1. First, open the Effects tab at the top of your screen.
2. In the Video Effects section, type "Mosaic" into the search bar.

3. Drag the mosaic effect onto your video clip in the timeline.
4. Adjust the length and position of the effect in the timeline to fit your needs.
5. To make any changes, just use the handles in the Preview Window to move and resize the blur as needed.

Click on the mosaic effect in the timeline to open the Effect Edit Panel. From there, you can choose the type of blur, adjust the opacity of the mosaic, and fine-tune the blur strength by sliding the preset settings.

Using Preset Templates in Filmora

Filmora's preset templates make editing faster by automatically adding elements like stickers, audio tracks, stock clips, and intro videos to your timeline. You can swap these out for your clips to add style to your project, and even adjust any decorative elements to suit your vision. These templates simplify post-production and save you from the hassle of fine-tuning every detail, improving your editing speed and efficiency.

Here's how to add a template to your timeline:

1. Click the Templates tab at the top of the screen.
2. You'll find a variety of templates on the left side, either under Mine or other categories. Scroll through and explore your options.
3. Click on any template to preview it before making your choice.
4. Once you've picked a template, simply drag it to the timeline to start using it in your project.

5. To bring in your media, start by selecting Project Media under the Media tab. Then, click the import icon to add your files. If you want to replace the default video, just import your media to do so.

6. To swap out the template footage, click the Provision button. When you click on the template, an advanced window will open. From there, you can drag and drop your clips to replace the ones in the template. Once you're happy with the changes, just click Save.

7. Simply click to preview your video and see how everything looks before finalizing your edits. This gives you a chance to make any last-minute tweaks or adjustments.

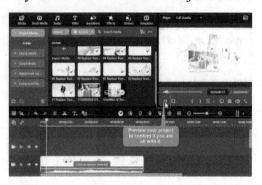

The Filmora Speed Property

Filmora gives you plenty of options to adjust the speed of your videos. You can slow down the footage to emphasize key moments or speed it up for a fun, fast-paced effect. Changing the speed at different points in the video adds dynamic interest, making it more engaging for viewers.

The Uniform Speed feature lets you set the entire selected clip to a consistent speed. Here's how to do it:

1. Select the clip in the timeline.

2. Click the Speed icon in the toolbar above the movie.

3. Choose the Uniform Speed option.

To set a steady pace for your video:

1. To speed up the video, slide the Speed slider to the right. To slow it down, move it to the left.

2. For more precise control over the speed, you can enter a specific value in the Duration area.

After adjusting the speed of your video, click the Play button in the Preview Window to see how your changes look. To keep the audio sounding natural, it's a good idea to enable the Maintain Audio Pitch option, which ensures the audio's tone stays consistent.

Speed Ramping

Speed ramping allows you to apply varying speeds to different parts of your clip, giving you more creative control. Unlike Uniform Speed, which applies the same speed throughout, Speed Ramping enables you to create smooth transitions between different speeds for a more dynamic effect.

Here's how to use it:

1. Click on the Speed icon (speedometer) above your timeline.
2. From the dropdown menu, select Speed Ramping.
3. Click on the clip to add speed points wherever you want the changes to occur.

128

4. To adjust the speed, simply drag the speed points up to speed up or down to slow it down.

5. Preview the video to check if the speed changes look just right.

6. To adjust the area affected by the speed change, just drag the speed point left or right. If you want to add a new speed point, move the playhead to the spot you want and click the Plus (+) symbol. To remove a speed point, simply click on it and hit the Minus (−) icon.

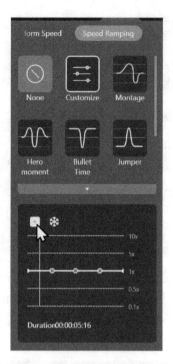

To change the speed using the clipping method:

1. Select the video clip in the timeline.
2. Hold down the Control (or Command on Mac) key, and move your mouse over the edge of the clip. This will show the speedometer and speed adjustment icon.
3. To adjust the playback speed, click and drag the edge of the clip left or right.

To see how the speed change impacts the scene, simply play the video. If needed, you can adjust the speed further until it looks just right.

CHAPTER 8

MASTERING AUDIO CLIPS IN FILMORA

We will explore the various tools and techniques Filmora offers to help you handle audio clips in your video projects. It covers the basics, like importing audio files, adding them to the timeline, and using split or trim functions for precise editing. You'll also learn how to apply audio effects, sync audio with video, and adjust audio levels to elevate the overall quality of your project. Additionally, the chapter explains how to export your final creation, ensuring that both your audio and visuals blend seamlessly. Mastering these skills will equip you to create captivating, high-quality video content.

How to Get Audio Clips

Filmora makes it super easy to add audio to your video projects. Whether you're pulling in music or sound effects from your computer, using royalty-free tracks from the stock library, recording voiceovers directly, or even turning text into speech, Filmora has you covered. With all these options, you'll have no trouble finding the perfect sound to bring your video to life.

1. Import Local Files: To bring audio files from your PC into the media library, just click on the "Import" option.
2. Stock Audio Library: Click on the "Audio" tab to explore Filmora's built-in collection of royalty-free music and sound effects.
3. Record Sounds: If you want to add voiceovers or other sounds, click the microphone button to record directly in Filmora.
4. Import from Other Projects: You can bring in audio from previous Filmora projects if needed.
5. Use External Libraries: You can also import audio from external sources that offer royalty-free music.

6. Extract from Video: To get audio from a video file, right-click on it in the timeline and select "Detach Audio."

7. Text-to-Audio: Use the text-to-audio tool to convert written text into spoken audio within Filmora.

Applying Your Audio Clips

To get started with audio in Filmora, you'll need to add your files to the media library first. You can either click the "Import" button to choose files from your computer or just drag and drop them into the library. Since Filmora supports multiple audio formats, you can easily use music, voiceovers, sound effects, and more.

1. **Import Your Audio:**

To import audio into Filmora, simply click the "Import" button in the media panel or go to the Media page. This will open up your computer, allowing you to find and select the audio files you want to use. Once imported, just drag and drop the audio clip onto the timeline, and you're ready to keep editing.

- **Stock Audio Library:** To find the perfect audio, go to the Audio option in the media menu and either scroll through or search for what you need. Once you've found the clip you want, just drag it to the timeline or click the "+" button to add it.

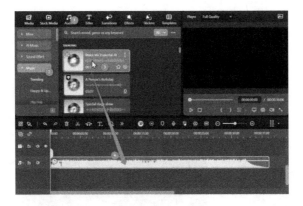

Turning Text into Speech:

Filmora's Text-to-Audio feature allows you to transform written text into lifelike speech. This makes it an excellent tool for adding voiceovers, commentary, or narration to your videos. Here's a simple guide to get you started:

1. Type the text you want to convert into speech.
2. Then, right-click on the text clip and select "Text to Speech" from the menu to open the necessary window for step 3.

3. Pick the voice type that suits your project, whether it's robotic, feminine, or male.
4. Tweak the volume, pitch, and speed to adjust the sound to your liking.

133

5. After you're satisfied, add the text to the timeline and convert it into audio.

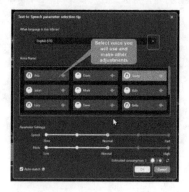

Audio Trimming and Splitting Techniques in Filmora

Filmora makes it easy to trim and split audio clips for precise editing. To trim a clip, simply hover your cursor over the edge of the audio on the timeline and drag it to shorten or extend the clip. If you want to split an audio clip, just grab the razor tool from the toolbar and click where you'd like to cut. This is great for smoothing transitions or removing unnecessary sections. Here's how to do it:

1. Click on the audio clip in the timeline.
2. When you move the playhead over the clip, the splitting icon will appear, or you can use the icon above the timeline.
3. To adjust the clip, drag the cursor to the start or end of the audio, depending on whether you want to shorten or lengthen it.

It's a simple way to fine-tune your audio to fit perfectly into your project!

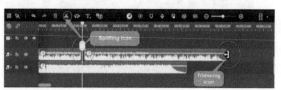

Adjusting Audio Levels in Filmora

Maintaining proper audio levels is essential for a professional finish. To adjust the audio levels, simply click on the audio clip in the timeline, then access the audio controls in the property panel on the right. This allows you to make dynamic adjustments throughout your project, including panning the audio and muffling certain sections. You can also apply fade-ins and fade-outs to ensure smooth transitions at the start and end of your audio clips.

Follow these steps to adjust the audio level:

1. Click on the audio clip to select it.
2. Hover over the "Audio" section in the attributes or edit window.
3. Move the slider forward or backward to adjust the volume.

When you closely observe the audio clip's waveform, you'll notice it rising and falling, signifying an increase or decrease in volume. To create smooth transitions, you can adjust the fade-in and fade-out of your audio.

Follow these steps to adjust the audio fade-in and fade-out:

1. Click on the audio clip in the timeline to select it.
2. Navigate to the Audio tab, where you'll find the Fade-in and Fade-out options.

3. Apply the fade effects, then preview your clip to ensure the changes were applied successfully.

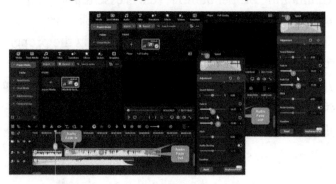

Audio Auto-Normalization in Filmora

The Auto Normalization tool automatically adjusts the loudness of each selected audio clip to 23.0 LUFS, the standard loudness level for European audio programs, with a deviation range of ±1 LU.

Follow these steps to apply Auto Normalization:

1. Hold down the Control key (or Command key on Mac) and select all the audio clips you want to adjust.
2. In the editing panel, locate and select the Auto Normalization option to apply the effect.
3. Preview your clips to ensure the adjustment has been applied correctly.

Optimizing Sound Levels in Filmora

Filmora's Sound Balance feature lets you adjust the audio between the left and right channels, giving you control over how sound is distributed across your project. For example, shifting the balance to the right will make the audio play only through the right side of your headphones. Here's how to adjust it:

1. Select the audio clip on the timeline.
2. In the editing window, use the balance slider to move the sound left or right and control how it's distributed.
3. For more precision, you can manually input a specific value to fine-tune the balance.

This feature gives you a simple way to create a more immersive and tailored sound experience in your video.

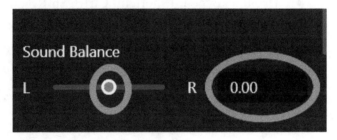

Synchronizing Video with Audio

To ensure your audio and video align perfectly, zoom in on the timeline for precise adjustments. This allows you to match specific audio elements, like dialogue or sound effects, with the corresponding moments in the video. The waveforms on the audio track act as a visual guide to help you sync audio cues with the visual actions. Take the time to arrange and cut the video as needed, and always review the project to ensure the audio and visuals are balanced and seamless. This will create a smooth and professional final product.

Muting the Entire Audio

You can mute the entire audio in four different ways:

- Use the keyboard shortcut: Ctrl + Shift + M.
- Click on the volume icon on the audio track.

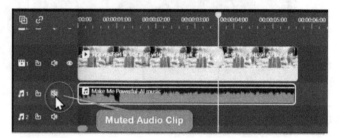

- Go to the upper menu bar and select **Tools > Audio > Mute**.
- Right-click on the video clip, then choose **Audio > Mute**.
- Use the **scissors** icon on the toolbar to split the audio, then select the audio clip and press **Ctrl + Shift + M** to mute it.

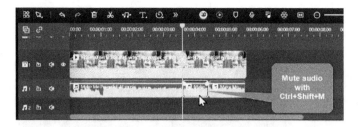

When you mute a clip, you'll notice that its volume meter appears darker compared to the others. This feature is often used in video editing to remove unwanted or offensive language. To mute the audio, simply apply the Mute feature. If you want to unmute it later, select the muted section and right-click to choose the Mute option again. Once you see that the checkmark is no longer there, the mute effect has been turned off.

Using Beat Detection in Filmora

Filmora's Beat Detection feature makes it super easy to sync your video edits with the rhythm of the music. It automatically picks up on the beats in your audio, which is great for creating videos that flow with the music, like vlogs, music videos, or promotional content.

Here's how you can use it:

1. Start by importing your audio file into the media pane.
2. Right-click on the audio and select Beat Detector.
3. Drag the audio clip onto your timeline.
4. You'll now see the beats marked, making it simple to line up your edits with the music.

Filmora's Beat Detection feature helps you effortlessly sync your video with the rhythm of the music by automatically identifying the beats in your audio.

Setting Up Beat Options

To adjust the beat detection settings, simply right-click on the song in your collection and choose "Beat Options." From there, you can tweak the Beat Model, Highlight Offset, Highlight Frequency, and the "Mark Beats Only" option to customize how the beats are displayed in your video.

Adjusting Beat Detection Settings

Here's how you can tweak the Beat Detection settings:

1. **Choosing Beat Model**: This setting allows you to highlight a specific drum beat or key rhythm that you want to focus on.
2. **Adjusting Highlight Frequency**: This controls how often the highlighted beats will appear, letting you match the rhythm with your video.
3. **Customizing Highlight Offset**: You can adjust the position of the highlighted beat, shifting it to different points in the track for better synchronization.
4. **Selecting Mark Highlight Beats Only**: When this option is checked, only the key beats will be highlighted. If unchecked, every beat will be marked in the audio track.

Adding Beat Markers

To add beat markers, follow these steps:

1. Select your audio file in the timeline.
2. Position the playhead where you want to place the marker.
3. Click the marker icon or press M on your keyboard to insert the beat marker.

This will help you sync your video with the beats more effectively.

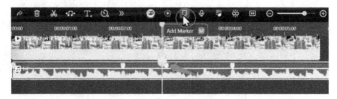

Removing Beat Markers

To remove beat markers from your video:

1. Right-click on the marker and select Delete, or simply select the marker and press the Delete key on your keyboard.

141

2. If you want to remove all beat markers at once, select Delete All Markers.

This will clean up your timeline if you need to start over or adjust your sync.

How to Separate Video and Audio

If you want to adjust or replace the audio without affecting the video, Filmora allows you to easily separate the two. Here's how:

1. Import Your Video: Start by adding your video to the timeline.
2. Right-click the Video: Right-click on the video clip within the timeline.
3. Select 'Detach Audio': Choose the "Detach Audio" option from the menu. This will separate the audio from the video.
4. Edit or Remove the Audio: Once detached, the audio will appear as a separate track, which you can move, modify, or delete as needed.

This feature is useful for making adjustments to the sound without altering the visuals of your video.

Adding and Applying Functional Audio Effects in Filmora

Filmora offers a range of built-in audio effects that you can apply to both audio and video clips to enhance the overall sound experience in your videos. These effects help you craft the perfect atmosphere or style for your project. Here's how to easily apply these effects:

1. Open Filmora and upload your video and audio files.
2. To edit the audio separately from the video, right-click on the video clip and select "Detach Audio."
3. Click on the "Audio" tab to explore the available audio effects.
4. From the effects menu, select the audio effect you want and apply it to the audio track.
5. Play the video to preview the effect, then tweak the timing and adjust the effect settings to fit your needs.

This simple process allows you to fine-tune your audio, creating a more immersive and dynamic experience for your viewers.

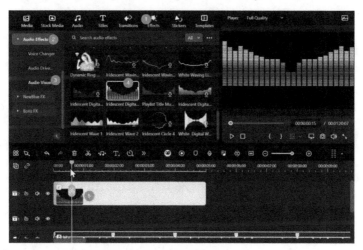

Adjusting Applied Audio Effects in Filmora

Filmora allows you to add and customize audio effects for your videos, giving you the ability to match the sound perfectly with the visuals. You can even add visual effects to your audio using the

Audio Visualizer feature. With over 25 audio visualizer options, Filmora makes it easy to find the one that fits your scene best. Here's how to modify your audio effects and explore various filters:

1. Add Visual Effects: Use the Audio Visualizer to add dynamic visual effects that respond to the audio. Simply drag and drop the effect, and Filmora will automatically sync it with your audio.
2. Customize Voice Filters: Filmora offers a range of voice filters, including Male Minion, Driving Sound, Large Room, Small Room, Echo, Lobby, and Phone. Each filter has its own set of parameters that can be adjusted to suit the mood and style you're going for.
3. Modify Effects: To fine-tune the applied effects, double-click the clip on the timeline, select the "Audio" tab, and click on "Audio Effects" to make adjustments.

Examples of Speech Filters:

- Big Room Effect: Creates the sensation of sound echoing through a large space. The higher you set it, the more the voice spreads throughout the room.
- Echo Effect: Adds a repeating sound effect, simulating an echo as if the sound is bouncing back from surfaces.
- Lobby Effect: Mimics the sound of speech echoing in a large lobby, making it seem distant and more spacious.
- Phone Effect: Recreates the unique sound of a phone call, with its characteristic muffled tones.
- Small Room Effect: Simulates the reverberation of sound in a small, enclosed space. The stronger the effect, the more noticeable the echo becomes.

With these customizable settings, Filmora gives you full control over how your audio sounds, allowing you to create the perfect atmosphere for your video.

Converting Audio to Text in Filmora

Audio-to-Text feature in Filmora enables you to convert audio from video or audio files into text captions or subtitles. This is a great way to boost audience engagement and make your content more accessible. Here's how you can use it:

1. Import Your Audio or Video: Start by importing the audio or video file you want to work with into Filmora.

2. Use the Voice-to-Text Function: Move your clips to the timeline, right-click on the audio file, and then scroll down the menu to select the voice-to-text option.

Once you click the "Speech to Text" option, a popup will appear, allowing you to make relevant adjustments.

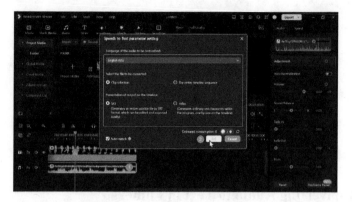

To confirm your selection, click "OK." Once done, the text will automatically appear on the timeline.

CHAPTER 9

REVOLUTIONIZING VIDEO EDITING WITH AI

AI has made video editing smarter and more accessible. Filmora's advanced tools take care of tasks like cutting, applying effects, and syncing audio, so creators can focus on what truly matters: storytelling. With AI handling the technical aspects, anyone can achieve professional-quality results in no time. This chapter delves into how Filmora simplifies and enhances the editing process, giving you the freedom to unleash your creativity.

Using the Smart Scene Cut Feature

Smart Scene Cut is a great tool for quickly capturing the best moments from a video. It's especially useful in the early stages of editing, as it automatically identifies key scenes, segments, and elements from long videos. Once the key moments are extracted, you can easily drag and drop them into your timeline for further editing, making it a breeze to create shorter videos.

Here's how to get started with Smart Scene Cut:

1. Begin by choosing the correct aspect ratio or video size. You can set this up when you first import your video from the launch page.

After that, locate the Smart Scene Cut feature within the editing tools.

1: On the launch page, you'll find two options for selecting the Smart Scene Cut feature. Clicking on either of them will bring up the Smart Scene Cut interface.

2: Another way is to import your video clips and then select "Smart Scene Cut" directly from the video thumbnail.

3: You can also right-click on the video clip and select "Smart Scene Cut" from the menu to open the interface for this specific feature.

- Once you click to open the Smart Scene Cut operation page, you'll be able to select up to ten objects for recognition. The tool will automatically extract the highlighted clips based on the objects you've chosen. After making your selections, simply click "Start" to begin the process.

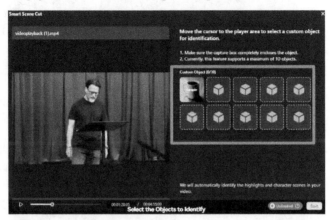

Note: You can select a maximum of ten objects for recognition.

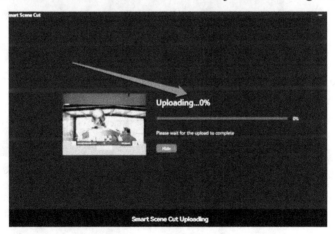

The smart upload is in progress now.

- Edit the entry and track progress. The "Task List > AI Creations Tasks" panel shows the status of the task, and you can click "Hide" to make the window disappear.

- To view the finished product, simply click the folder icon in the top-left corner of the video in the "Media Folder."

To open the edit page, just double-click on the video with your mouse.

Note: If you don't click "Hide" during the generation process, the result preview page will automatically appear on your screen.

1. Review the Final Results: The Smart Scene Cut results page displays three categories: "Character Scene," "Highlight Scene," and "Custom Object."

- Highlight Scene: This feature helps identify key highlight moments in your video. You can select and add these highlighted segments to the timeline, allowing you to refine the main track further.

- Character Scene: This feature intelligently detects and highlights important moments involving characters, making it easier to focus on the key scenes for your video.

- Character Object: You can also capture custom elements within your video. Filmora will track and highlight the relevant clips that feature these custom objects throughout the entire video.

- Adjust the Main Timeline: Once you've selected all your scenes, simply click "Edit in the Main Timeline" to begin working on them in the main editing timeline.

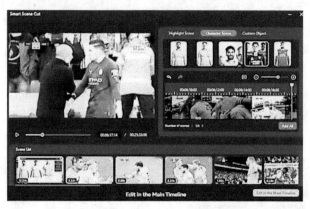

- Tailor your highlight clips in the main timeline to fit your creative vision. You can add text, sound effects, transitions, and other elements to enhance your video.

- Once you've chosen a destination, select "MP4" or your preferred video format. Make any adjustments to the export settings, then click "Export" to save your video.

Working with Smart Short Clips:

Want to turn your long videos into quick, attention-grabbing clips for social media? Filmora's Smart Short Clips feature makes it super easy! In just a few clicks, this handy tool automatically picks out the most important moments in your footage, so you can create engaging shorts without all the hassle. Keep reading to find out how!

Accessing the Smart Short Clips Feature:

1. From the Main Page: When you open Filmora, you'll find the Smart Short Clips option in the New Project menu.

2. Accessing Through Filmora Cloud: You can also open Smart Short Clips through Filmora Cloud. Just click on the Filmora Cloud icon, and you'll find the Smart Short Clips option under the general Cloud Space tools.

3. Accessing Through the Toolbox: Navigate to the Toolbox section. You can either explore the latest new features or

locate the Smart Short Clips option directly within the function cards.

How to Use Smart Short Clips:

Step 1: Upload Your Footage

You can either paste a link to your own YouTube video, upload a video file directly from your device, or select a file stored in Filmora Cloud.

Note: If you're using a YouTube URL, make sure it's content you own.

When you upload a video, you'll need to manually choose the source language. If you prefer not to stick with the default settings, you can also customize the Duration and Themes to fit your needs.

To set the aspect ratio and let Smart BGM Generation automatically create music that fits your content, head to the Advanced option. *Tip:* You can add a few keywords in the Main Topic box to help the AI create animations that match your material better

There are plenty of great templates available across different themes. Just scroll down to browse the selection of short movie templates, choose the one you like, and click Generate to get started.

The software will take some time to detect the language of the video source and upload it.

The system will produce several results and assign a rating according to the platform's guidelines.

Step 2: Choose Your Shorts

During the generation process, you can click "Generate Offline" to leave the current page and work on your other videos. You'll also receive an email notification once it's generated.

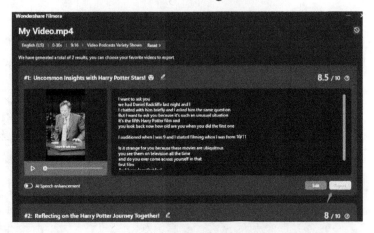

Tips: You can click Reset to regenerate the content if needed. To improve your voice recordings beyond simple denoising, enable AI Speech Enhancement. Once you've selected your preferred video snippets, you can either refine them further or export them directly.

Step 3: Edit Your Video:

By clicking Edit, you'll access the Smart Short Clips editing screen. You can then review the script by timecode for more straightforward editing in Time Code Mode or select which captions to display or hide in Select Mode.

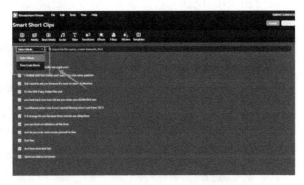

Note: Selecting the correct location also allows you to create and edit thumbnails.

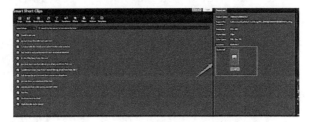

Select the clip and head over to the **Text** tab to adjust the font style so it better matches your video's theme. When you're happy with it, just click **Apply to All** to apply the changes throughout the whole video.

You'll find a wide range of extra templates and resources for titles, transitions, effects, filters, and stickers in the top toolbar. To edit the text, go to the Text tab and select the Basic option. From there, you can highlight certain words, merge text, or make any changes you need.

If you're not satisfied with the current voice or want to add more dialogue to your video, you can use the Text-to-Speech feature to create new voiceovers from your text.

You can also zoom in or out, delete stickers, and make other adjustments to the final video.

The AI will automatically recognize the characters based on the given conditions and place them in the center using a balanced split-screen layout.

Step 4: Export Your Shorts

Once the Export window opens, choose the social media platform you want to upload your video to (like YouTube, TikTok, Instagram, Facebook, or Vimeo). You can also adjust settings such as the title, description, category, resolution, and more before publishing.

If you want to schedule your post, simply turn on the Schedule option and set your preferred date and time.

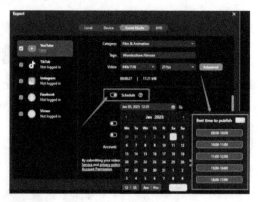

AI Video Enhancer

With just one click, you can instantly boost the clarity of your original video, making it a quick and easy way to upgrade video quality. AI Video Enhancer is especially useful for videos that are blurry or lacking detail, often due to being filmed with old, low-resolution devices or dirty lenses.

Here's how you can enhance your video quality:

1. Import your media files and add them to the timeline. Start by bringing your video clips into Wondershare Filmora and placing them on the timeline.

Note: There are some limitations based on the length of the video clip and media resolution. For videos with a resolution of 1080P or higher, the clip must be one minute or shorter. For videos with a resolution of 1080P or lower, the clip should be three minutes or less.

2. Double-click on the clip in the timeline to open the editing panel. Go to Video > AI Tools and click the button next to AI Video Enhancer to activate it. After that, click Generate, and the system will start analyzing and processing your video.

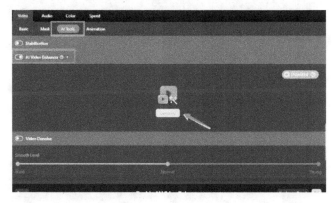

During this process, the clip in the timeline will be grayed out, preventing it from being selected or moved. If you click on it, a task interruption dialog will appear.

3. Once the process is complete, the enhanced clip will automatically appear in the media section.

Click Play to preview the results in the preview box. The HD version will also be added to the timeline automatically.

Once you're done editing, click Export and choose the format you'd like to save the final video in.

Filmora's Image-to-Video Feature

With Filmora's Image to Video feature, you can easily transform still photos into engaging videos. The tool allows you to add dynamic effects and transitions, bringing your images to life with just a few clicks, thanks to its variety of themes and customizable options.

How to Use Filmora's Image to Video Feature:

1: Easy Access from the Main Interface: When you open Filmora, the AI Image to Video tool is located in the Toolbox section on the home screen, where it appears as the first option.

2: Via the Toolbox: If Image to Video isn't visible on the home screen, simply go to the Toolbox in the left-hand sidebar. Once there, find and select the Image to Video tool to begin using it.

3: Using the Editing Interface Media Tab: Once you've created a new project, head over to the Media tab at the top of the editor. In the left sidebar, find Image to Video under Media, and click Start Creating to get started.

How to Make the Most of the Image-to-Video Feature in Filmora:

To create beautiful videos with your selected template, simply open the Image to Video tool and follow the steps provided. Note: The process remains the same across all templates, with only minor differences in the outcomes.

1: Pick a Template: Explore the different templates in the Image to Video section. Each template is designed for a unique mood or effect:

- **AI Fight**: Use dramatic AI effects to create intense battle scenes.
- **AI Kiss**: Add a romantic touch with AI-generated effects.
- **Custom**: Personalize your video by uploading an image and describing your artistic vision.
- **Horror**: Craft eerie videos with unsettling and spooky effects.
- **Hug Your Love**: Create emotional and heartfelt visuals.
- **Painting Fugitive**: Transform your photos into imaginative, escape-themed stories.
- **Sandify**: Add a dreamy atmosphere with soft, sand-like fade effects.
- **Smoke Escape**: Create a mysterious vibe with dramatic, hazy visuals.
- **Struck by Lightning**: Energize your images with striking lighting effects.

Once you've selected a template, click Create to proceed.

2: Choose a Template: Browse through the templates in the Image to Video section. Each one is designed to fit a specific mood or effect:

- **AI Fight**: Use dramatic effects to create intense battle scenes.
- **AI Kiss**: Add a romantic touch with AI-generated effects.
- **Custom**: Upload an image and share your vision to create a personalized film.
- **Horror**: Create eerie, unsettling videos with spooky effects.
- **Hug Your Love**: Capture emotional, heartwarming moments with touching visuals.
- **Painting Fugitive**: Transform your photos into imaginative escape-themed stories.
- **Sandify**: Add soft, sand-like fade effects for a dreamy vibe.
- **Smoke Escape**: Create mysterious and dramatic visuals with hazy effects.
- **Struck by Lightning**: Energize your images with powerful lightning effects.

Once you've picked a template, simply click Create to move forward.

3: Preview the Template and Upload Your Photos: Once you select a template, a preview of its effects will appear in the player on the right, helping you visualize the final result before continuing.

165

You can easily add your photos by either clicking to browse your files or dragging and dropping them into the upload box.

In the Custom template, enter a clear explanation of the effect you want to achieve. For example, you might say, "Produce a timelapse showing this bridge transitioning from day to night."

4: Customize Your Photos: You can choose from several modes:

- **Single Image**: Focus on one image and make it stand out.
- **Stitch Mode**: Combine multiple photos to create a seamless video.

At the top, select either 16:9 (landscape) or 9:16 (portrait) to adjust the video's resolution. Once you're happy with your settings, click Submit to confirm your choices and move on to the next step.

5: Create the Video: Once you've uploaded your photos and made your adjustments, click Generate to begin creating your video. The AI will process your inputs, and you'll see a progress bar as it works.

Depending on your selections, the video creation may take anywhere from a few seconds to a few minutes.

Here's a preview of the final results for the 'Hug Your Love' template.

After your video is generated, it will appear in the 'My File' section of the Image to Video tool. Select it, and it will open in the Player panel on the right. You can then drag and drop the video onto the Timeline to make further edits. Once you're satisfied with your adjustments, click the 'Export' button located in the upper-right corner.

CONCLUSION

As we wrap up our exploration of Wondershare Filmora's video editing features, it's clear that this powerful tool offers plenty of creative possibilities. Whether you're a beginner or an experienced editor, Filmora provides a simple platform with lots of options to enhance your work. This guide aims to give you the essentials, from importing files and basic editing to more advanced features like motion tracking and audio adjustments.

Throughout this journey, we've learned that mastering the tools at your disposal is key. Each chapter was designed to walk you through the steps, from setting up your workspace to using advanced tools that can take your projects to the next level. Remember, practice is the key to getting better. The more you experiment with Filmora, the better you'll get at turning your creative ideas into amazing videos.

And don't forget the power of storytelling as you improve your skills. Video editing is more than just cutting and rearranging clips—it's about sharing ideas, emotions, and messages. With Filmora, you have the tools to create content that resonates with your audience.

We hope this guide has helped you along your editing journey. Don't hesitate to share your unique story with the world, embrace your creativity, and keep learning. Enjoy editing!

Filmora Shortcuts Keys

Here's a table with the Filmora Keyboard Shortcuts and their descriptions:

Shortcut	Action	Mac Shortcut
Add a New Scene	Adds a new scene to your project	Cmd + N
Add a New Title	Adds a new title to your project	Cmd + T
Copy	Copies the selected item	Cmd + C
Cut	Cuts the selected item	Cmd + B
Delete	Deletes the selected item	Delete key
Go to End	Jumps to the end of the timeline	End
Go to Start	Jumps to the start of the timeline	Home
Paste	Pastes the copied or cut item	Cmd + V
Play/Pause	Plays or pauses the video	Spacebar
Redo	Redoes the last undone action	Cmd + Shift + Z
Stop	Stops playback of the video	K
Toggle Full Screen	Toggles full screen mode	Cmd + F
Undo	Undoes the last action	Cmd + Z
Zoom In	Zooms in on the timeline	Cmd + +
Zoom Out	Zooms out on the timeline	Cmd + -

INDEX

171

www.ingramcontent.com/pod-product-compliance
Lightning Source LLC
La Vergne TN
LVHW022346060326
832902LV00022B/4281